CROSS-COUNTRY CHRONICLES

Road Trips Through the Art and Soul of America

by Arthur D. Hittner

Reprint Edition © 2017 by Arthur D. Hittner. All rights reserved.
ISBN 978-0-9989810-2-4

© 2012 by Arthur D. Hittner. All rights reserved. No part of this publication may be reproduced or transmitted in any form or by any means, electronic or mechanical, including photocopying, recording or any other information storage or retrieval system, without permission in writing from the author.

Published in U.S.A. by Apple Ridge Fine Arts Press, a division of Apple Ridge Fine Arts, 20 South Avenue #304, Natick, MA 01760.

First printing, February, 2013.

Front cover illustration: Primitive cowboy on steriods outside Dalhart, Texas. Author photo.

Rear cover illustration: An intersection near Lusk, Wyoming. Author photo.

All photographs are by the author.

The Blurb-provided layout designs and graphic elements are copyright Blurb Inc., 2012. This book was created using the Blurb creative publishing service. The book author retains sole copyright to his or her contributions to this book.

Contents

Prologue 5

Trip One: The Duct Tape Diaries 6

Garbage In, Garbage Out: The Adventure Begins
Tucson to Show Low, AZ 7
Nowhere to Noplace
Show Low, AZ to Albuquerque, NM 11
The Tale of the (Duct) Tape
Albuquerque, NM to Liberal, KS 15
No Puking or Leaking
Liberal to Wichita, KS 19
The Plains Drifters
Wichita, KS to Columbia, MO 21
Last Room in the Daze Inn
Columbia, MO to Terra Haute, IN 23
Indianapolis is OK by Me
Terre Haute to Indianapolis, IN 26
A Day in the Country
Indianapolis, IN to Granville, OH 28
Half-Cooked in Uniontown
Granville, OH to Uniontown, PA 31
Aunt Carol, Uncle Herb and the C.I.A.
Uniontown, PA to Poughkeepsie, NY 35
Duct Tape Denouement
Poughkeepsie, NY to Natick, MA 39

Trip Two: God, Guns and the Rump at the Pump ... 40

The Electric Cow Paddy
Natick, MA to Stephens City, VA 41
Two Toilets and Three Art Museums
Stephens City, VA to Mobile, AL 45
Guns, Jesus and the "Big Easy"
Mobile, AL to New Orleans, LA 49
Dust, Duct Tape, Temptation, God and Guns
New Orleans, LA to Pecos, TX 52
Rump at the Pump
Pecos, TX to Tucson, AZ 56

Trip Three: Take the Long Way Home　　　　　　　　　　*58*

On the Road Again
　　Tucson to Flagstaff, AZ　　　　　　　　　　　　　　　*59*
Hittners Survive Grand Canyon Drive-by
　　Grand Canyon, AZ　　　　　　　　　　　　　　　　　*61*
Eggs, Mermaids and The Sin City
　　Flagstaff, AZ to Las Vegas, NV　　　　　　　　　　　*64*
Where Chocolate Flows and Romney Glows
　　Las Vegas, NV to Zion National Park, UT　　　　　　*67*
Blowin' Through Wyomin'
　　Zion National Park, UT to Laramie, WY　　　　　　　*69*
Sexy Tractors and Crazy Horses
　　Laramie, WY to Rapid City, SC　　　　　　　　　　　*71*
Wall Drug Wonders and the Flying Trashcan
　　Rapid City to Sioux Falls, SD　　　　　　　　　　　　*76*
Roadkill and Other Norwegian Treats
　　Sioux Falls, SD to Milwaukee, WI　　　　　　　　　　*79*
Milwaukee in Drag
　　Milwaukee, WI to South Bend, IN　　　　　　　　　　*82*
Not Quite Shaker Heights
　　South Bend, IN to Cleveland, OH　　　　　　　　　　*84*
Big Al, Rock & Roll and the Institution
　　Cleveland, OH to Chautauqua, NY　　　　　　　　　　*87*
Bronco Busting
　　Chautauqua to Ithaca, NY　　　　　　　　　　　　　　*90*
Home Again!
　　Ithaca, NY to Natick, MA　　　　　　　　　　　　　　*92*

Trip Four: Copulating Cabs and Little Green Men　　　　*93*

Drought Busting and Fat Lady Lusting
　　Natick, MA to Potomac, MD　　　　　　　　　　　　　*94*
Midwestern Daze: Politically Incorrect in Appalachia
　　Potomac, MD to Mt. Vernon, IL　　　　　　　　　　　*98*
A Butt of a Different Color
　　Mt. Vernon, IL to St. Louis, MO　　　　　　　　　　　*101*
(Washing) Hands Across America (or Why Did the Cubans Steal My Sink?)
　　St. Louis, MO to Eureka Springs, AR　　　　　　　　*105*
Tales from Bentonville (or How I Was Outbid by a Walmart Heiress)
　　Eureka Springs, AR to Tulsa, OK　　　　　　　　　　*108*
Copulating Cabs
　　Tulsa, OK to Clovis, NM　　　　　　　　　　　　　　*112*
Little Green Men and Useless Las Cruces
　　Clovis to Deming, NM　　　　　　　　　　　　　　　　*118*
We're Back in Tucson
　　Deming, NM to Tucson, AZ　　　　　　　　　　　　　*121*

Prologue

From Kerouac to Steinbeck, the cross-country road trip has ranked highly among the more celebrated of literary rituals. Absent the relentless demands of work and family, who among us would fail to leap at the opportunity to hop behind the wheel and hit the old gas pedal on a pilgrimage along interstates and two-lane country roads in search of America? In the three years since my retirement at the end of 2009, my wife and I have made seven such trips between seasonal residences in metropolitan Boston and Tucson, Arizona, embarking in each case on a different itinerary in our quest to observe and explore the physical wonders and oddities and to experience the cultural diversity of our great nation. What began in 2010 as an occasional email to family and friends from various points along our route had grown by 2012 to a more considered daily or near-daily journal and commentary to an ever-burgeoning distribution list. Written with what to some may appear to be a dry wit (and others something more insidious), the entries and accompanying photos tell the story of America as we've experienced it, in all of its glorious (or inglorious) aspects. They also document, in frequently mind-numbing detail, the trials and tribulations of the road. This chronicle is not recommended for the faint-of-heart, or (for that matter) Republicans. Like the umpire with three-inch thick glasses, I calls 'em as I sees 'em, with biases intact. That being said, I fervently hope you'll enjoy reading, as much as I did writing, the chronicles of our four most recent trans-American road trips.

Arthur D. Hittner
January 28, 2013

Trip One

The Duct Tape Diaries

**Oro Valley (Tucson), Arizona to Natick, Massachusetts
12 Days, 2,850 Miles
May 23-June 3, 2011**

Garbage In, Garbage Out: The Adventure Begins

Day 1 (Monday, May 23, 2011): Tucson to Show Low, AZ (185 miles)

We left our Oro Valley house this morning with a car full of crap, literally. In addition to four suitcases and a variety of bags and boxes, we brought two garbage bags filled with, of all things, our garbage. Since discontinuing our waste removal service for the season, we had to find someplace to deposit our last three days of trash. So the first stop on the trip was our local golf course where one of the employees whom we'd befriended graciously agreed to relieve us of our garbage! Great start!

On to the roadway for about 100 yards, then a stop for breakfast. Can't travel on an empty stomach and no food left in the house!

OK, an hour into the trip and we're 3 minutes from home. So, satiated with french toast, we finally hit the road for real. Heading north, it takes only about 20 miles for all signs of civilization to disappear. We drive a two-lane roadway through lovely mountains and valleys. Halfway to our day's destination, we pull in to the old mining town of **Globe, Arizona**. It is in the middle of nowhere (and mired in the 1950s). Clearly it has seen better days. The photos appearing

Two examples of the old signage in the partially abandoned downtown of Globe, Arizona

above show a sampling of old signage in the half-inhabited downtown. We pass an old drive-in movie theater on the road out of town; it looks to still be operational!

From Globe we drive northeast through the gorgeous **Salt River Canyon** (see photo on the following page). The roadway winds dizzyingly along the canyon walls as we marvel at the scenery. The entire trip today is on two-lane country roads. We continue to climb through mountains until, suddenly, pine forests appear and dominate the landscape. About twenty minutes later, we pull into the Holiday Inn Express in **Show Low**. Should have kept going as there is nothing doing here. It is windy and, at 6,400 feet of elevation, about 20 degrees cooler than it was when we left Tucson. The good news, though, is that the Red Sox are on ESPN (4 PM our time) so I'm happy. Uh, oh. Rain delay at the ballpark. Could be a long evening...

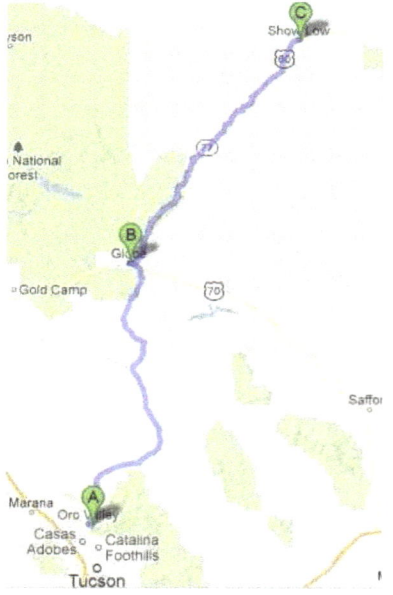

The mandatory local gun shop in Globe, Arizona

Peggy admires the Salt River Canyon

Speed Traps and Stray Cats: A Postscript from Globe

A (not very) funny thing happened to us several weeks after our visit to Globe. We received a rather unwelcome gift in the mail: a citation for allegedly driving at the bone-rattling speed of 46 mph in a sleepy 35 mph zone, a speed deemed "greater than reasonable and prudent". The citation was accompanied by four photos showing our car hurtling along the four-lane highway just outside town at the spine-tingling speed alleged. With our out-of-state license plates, we were an easy mark for the local authorities for whom the unmarked speed trap is likely their primary source of government funding. According to the mailing, my options were to admit guilt and pay the ludicrous fine of $206 or to fly to Globe within the next 60 days and defend myself in a kangaroo court against my electronic accuser. If I elected to defend myself, it appeared that I would have to face a judge who, according to the Arizona Republic, had "been suspended for 30 days without pay after he used a city credit card to pay for car repairs and buy vaccines for a stray cat." This apparently explains why this particular jurist had been assigned to do his penance by presiding in the Magistrate Court in the barren frontier town of Globe, and this entire experience explains why we'll likely never visit this ----ing burb again.

Nowhere to Noplace

Day 2 (Tuesday, May 24, 2011): Show Low, AZ to Albuquerque, NM (285 miles)

We left the metropolis of **Show Low, Arizona** around 8 AM, having first gorged on our spartan continental breakfast at the Holiday Inn Express. If nothing else, it's convenient. It's chilly here in the mountains, in the upper 40's (I know that's nothing for you New Englanders but for we Arizonans it's unsettling!)

Five minutes north of Show Low we encounter two-lane roads spanning the distance from Nowhere to Noplace. Absolutely nothing but scenery; no cars to pass, only a handful coming past in the opposite direction. Except for an occasional ranch, there is barely a trace of humanity for miles. We enjoy the subtly changing landscape as we proceed northeast, rising gently in elevation until we reach about 7,500 feet. You can drive at whatever speed you desire, as there are few turns and no cops *[I obviously wrote this before the Global Attack described on the preceding page]*. There isn't even any roadkill!

Well into the second hour of our two-lane ecstasy, we head through Indian territory as we cross into **New Mexico** and proceed east to the **Zuni Pueblo**, ancestral home of the Zunis (duh!). The Zuni Pueblo is essentially a town of about 6,000 Zuni people, mostly housed in rundown homes, many of what appears to be old adobe construction. We visit the Visitors Center and a couple of trading posts or artists' cooperatives along the main street (after getting lost in search of a small local museum). We take no photos, as photography is forbidden

A view of El Morro National Monument

without a permit (which can be purchased in the Visitors Center for $10). To prove we aren't cheapskates, though, we leave town with a beautiful silver belt buckle for Art. Pretty much an impulse purchase but really neat. Seemed more likely to get used than the bolo ties we looked at (after all, you need a way to keep your pants on). All I need is a belt to attach it to. Peggy winds up with nothing because her wrist and fingers are too small to qualify for Native American jewelry. Bummer.

A bit further down the road we encountered the **El Morro National Monument**. Rather than bullshit like I know what it was I'll insert here a paragraph from Wikipedia telling you all you need to know:

El Morro National Monument is located on an ancient east-west trail in western New Mexico. The main feature of this National Monument is a great sandstone promontory with a pool of water at its base. As a shaded oasis in the western U.S. desert, this site has seen many centuries of travelers. The remains of a mesa top pueblo are atop the promontory where between about 1275 to 1350 AD, up to 1500 people lived in this 875-room pueblo. The Spaniard explorers called it El Morro (The Headland). The Zuni Indians call it "A'ts'ina" (Place of writings on the rock). Anglo-Americans called it Inscription Rock. Travelers left signatures, names, dates, and stories of their treks. While some of the inscriptions are fading, there are still many that can be seen today, some dating to the 17th century. Some petroglyphs and carvings were made by the Anasazi centuries before Europeans started making their mark. In 1906, U.S. federal law prohibited further carving.

We stopped at the National Park Service's Visitor Center and watched a 15-minute movie. Peggy nodded off (me too, I'll sheepishly admit). Actually, though, it was pretty neat—especially the inscriptions on the rock which (as noted above) date from time immemorial through the Spanish Conquest to 1906 when the feds decided enough graffiti already. The lonely NPS officers were basically pleading with us (perhaps the day's only visitors) to take the hike from the Visitors Center to the rock promontory to see the graffiti but, as you can probably tell, we were too tired (and it was relatively cold and super windy, among other excuses).

From El Morro we continued east, reaching Interstate 40 by lunchtime. For the first time in decades, we stopped at a McDonald's for something other than Peggy's going to the ladies room. Neither is an experience worthy of further comment.

The last 75 miles of today's journey was a straight shot of interstate to

A photo of the resident white peacock at the Los Poblanos Inn, Albuquerque, New Mexico

A view of the grounds at Los Poblanos Inn, Albuquerque, New Mexico

Albuquerque, New Mexico. It was the first taste of interstate on our trip and not nearly as enjoyable as the two-lane highways through nowheresville. More vehicles passed in the first five minutes than we had seen in the last two days combined.

We arrived at the **Los Poblanos Inn** in Albuquerque where we had stayed on our trip out here last fall. It is a gracious old hacienda-style bed and breakfast with a working lavender farm (among other crops), animals, farmstand and other facilities. Really nice place decorated with antique Mexican and New Mexican folk art and furniture. It also boasts a separate house with 1930s murals (which we toured on our last visit).

I'm writing this in the library of the inn as I endure mild indigestion emanating from dinner at **Johndi's BBQ** which was actually pretty good. Peggy's back in the room watching *American Idol*.

We head off tomorrow morning on the interstate across the rest of New Mexico and then northeast on the state highway which takes us through the northwest corner of the Texas panhandle, across the Oklahoma panhandle and then into Kansas. Wichita is the next major destination but too far for one day so we'll stop somewhere where we can find a modicum of civilization when we get tired of driving. Watching the weather forecasts as it appears we are about a day or two behind the tornadoes and other severe weather expected tonight in Wichita and other areas around it. Hoping for the best...

The Tale of the (Duct) Tape

Day 3 (Wednesday, May 25, 2011): Albuquerque, NM to Liberal, KS (385 miles)

We departed **Albuquerque** on a full stomach, compliments of the Los Poblanos Inn. Huevos rancheros, fresh squeezed OJ and we're ready to go tornado chasing (or NOT!). The wind is kicking up substantially, but the really horrible weather is a day or two ahead of us and a heat wave is a day or two behind. Hoping to stay safely and comfortably in between...

Our day starts with three hours of driving across **New Mexico** on Interstate 40. BORING. Lots of trucks. Peggy's bored enough to do stretching exercises in the passenger seat, a feat possible only for those of Peggy's minimal stature. About 175 miles later, we gladly depart the interstate for what we're hoping is another joyous day of two-lane highway bliss through the **Texas** and **Oklahoma** panhandles and into southwestern **Kansas**.

Well, at least we got the two-lane highway. U.S. 54 runs on a straight shot to the northeast. On the way, we bore ourselves silly. Train track on the right, endless and unremarkable farmland on both sides. Traffic is minimal but mostly long-haul tractor-trailers. Our main entertainment is revving it up to 85 to pass a truck every 20 miles or so. Yippee! A few puny towns along the road serve the truckers and grain elevators pop up periodically along the rail line. One of the larger towns,

This primitive cowboy on steroids was on the roadside outside Dalhart, Texas. Not connected to any present business or activity; just there, in the middle of nowhere

Dalhart (in the Texas panhandle), announces its presence with a generous dose of methane. The smell of cow manure permeates the next five miles. At least it's a change... Two-lane highways are not all created equal, it seems.

We pass by our first candidate for the day's destination (**Guymon, OK**). Not much more than a glorified (in relative terms, mind you) truckstop. So it's another 40 miles to **Liberal, Kansas**. I don't imagine for a second there are any liberals here. By now the wind has whipped up to at least 40 mph, with constant gusts. Feels like Oz. In fact, I think it is— they have a **Dorothy's House/Land of Oz** museum here (no kidding!). No signs of seriously bad weather, though. We get lost in Liberal, but eventually find our way to a Holiday Inn Express (seems safe). We pull into the parking lot and hear a funny dragging sound. Naturally, we dismiss it.

After checking in, I return to the car and notice a big flap of plastic protruding to the ground from beneath the front undercarriage of the vehicle. A bolt may have

A train runs along the track beside our two-lane roadway. This was as good as it gets

I was mighty proud of my duct-tape handiwork fastening the undercarriage to the front bumper

broken off and this plastic undercarriage protector has torn away. We drive to a Walmart lube and tire department where we plead for any help the guy there can give us. Displaying the hospitality of a typical Midwesterner, he shimmies under the front of the car to inspect the damage. This man is about 275 pounds and his girth prevents him from making his way terribly far beneath the car. Nevertheless, he wedges himself in there and presses the plastic into place. Then, much to my amazement and relief (and against all odds), he successfully extricates himself from beneath the car. Looks serviceable, so we thank him profusely and hop back into the car.

When we return to the hotel, I take another look underneath the car. I figure if he could fit, so can I. Still looks sketchy. I then walk a couple blocks through what are now probably 50 mph gusts to a hardware store and buy a roll of duct tape and a pair of scissors. Returning to the hotel parking lot, I whip out my roll of duct tape and randomly apply as much as I can. The undercarriage is now duct-taped to the front bumper. Looks classy. Hopefully, we're ready to roll to Wichita tomorrow! Pray for us.

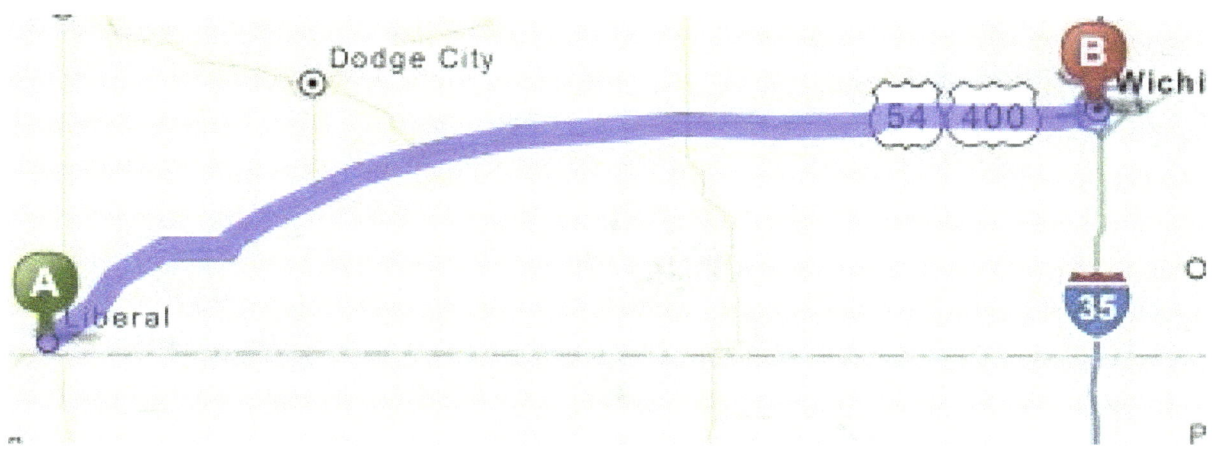

No Puking or Leaking

Day 4 (Thursday, May 26, 2011): Liberal, KS to Wichita, KS (200 miles)

Breakfast again compliments of the Holiday Inn. Not gourmet but the price is right. Eager to see if the duct tape holds….

As we leave the inaptly named City of Liberal, Kansas, we are roundly assaulted by a raucous stench as we follow a cattle truck past the National Beef rendering plant. Both plant and odor are monstrous. Ugh!

We return to the two-lane highway which continues its relentless path northeast along the railroad tracks. Once again, we find ourselves frequently trailing tractor-trailers. I engineer more 85 mph passes than Peggy can stomach. But it keeps us moving and we (fortunately) survive. The towns are a little more closely spaced, each featuring its own railside grain elevator, gas station and feed store. More than one-third of the traffic is of the large truck variety. I don't give much thought to my duct-taped undercarriage and it seems to be holding up (literally).

We just keep plodding along today, hoping to reach **Wichita** by lunchtime, and we do. We head right for the **Wichita Art Museum**, which is our only planned activity of the day. We are not disappointed, as it is a very nice museum of mostly American art, with a smattering of works from the Thirties and Forties. It also boasts a good café where we enjoy a nice lunch. As we leave the museum, we ask the superannuated desk clerk about possible walks in the area. She lives behind the museum but can't seem to figure out where we are or how to get around. She does offer us a map and we take it.

We enjoy an hour and a half walking in and around the riverfront where this and other museums are located. We eye a tern (?), ducks with young ducklings, a swimming snake, some homeless people and some floating trash. We even spy the Wichita minor league baseball stadium but determine that the team is away for the day. Peggy is relieved. We get our exercise walking and are pleased.

Fortunately, we relocate the duct-tape mobile and drive about a mile to the **Castle Inn Bed & Breakfast**. It is supposed to have free wifi and an internet special of $25 off. When we arrive we find out that the free wifi doesn't work and there is no breakfast (I guess that's what the $25 discount is all about). We're also required to sign an occupancy agreement which basically says we won't puke on anything, stain anything or leak on anything in the room *or else* (not necessarily their words but a fair summary). The place is virtually unhosted and we're virtually alone (though there is supposed to be one other guest) in this massive dozen-or-so room Victorian castle. The inn is physically appealing but the artwork is enough to cause you to violate the occupancy agreement all over the rug.

We have dinner at a decent place a few miles away and I check out the car's undercarriage when we get back. I give it a fresh dressing of duct tape and we retire to our room in the bed and (no) breakfast.

No photos today as there wasn't anything even remotely photogenic. We are off tomorrow for Columbia, Missouri.

The Plains Drifters

Day 5 (Friday, May 27, 2011): Wichita, KS to Columbia, MO (325 miles)

We got up, got ourselves together in our tiny top-floor room in the least charming castle in Wichita, said our goodbyes to no one and left the otherwise empty and thoroughly unhosted bed and (no) breakfast as soon as we could. We shared three pancakes at a café with (naturally) no wifi and, after checking the security of our duct-taped undercarriage, hit the road again. Today's trip took us north from Wichita to (almost) Kansas City and then west from (almost) KC to **Columbia, Missouri**. The Missouri portion of the trip took us past several towns which we had traversed by bicycle two years earlier when we rode the **Katy Trail** from just outside of St. Louis to the outskirts of Kansas City. Brought back memories of a really sore ass.

Today the ride was mostly uneventful. There was some beautiful scenery on the northern leg of the trip where endless rolling green hills are dotted (and besotted) by lazy herds of cattle. Constantly keeping ourselves abreast of the weather reports on our iPhone, we are relieved to find the forecast favorable. The first drops appeared on our windshield shortly thereafter. It was, of course, the first rain to grace our Arizona-garaged vehicle for six months and since we never cleaned it, it was certainly due. It proceeded to rain for a couple of hours but (fortunately) the duct tape continued to hold. When we needed a break we picked up some iced tea at a McDonald's and were delighted to discover that MickeyDs have wifi. Who knew? That gave us a chance to fill all your e-mailboxes with the accumulated poop on the last couple of days of our journey.

We arrived in **Columbia** in the mid-afternoon. This is a very neat college town, home to the **University of Missouri** and two other colleges we've never heard of. With a modicum of trepidation resulting from last night's experience, we checked into another bed and breakfast. This one is hosted, wi-fied and serves breakfast! No occupancy agreements to sign! This is actually in the midst of fraternity row (fraternities on both sides) as it is owned by the university and run by its Department of Agriculture as a hospitality training facility. Since school is out, there's nothing doing next door on Friday night but our B&B is still manned by students and supervised by a live-in host of our vintage. How nice! Room is amazing. We lose ourselves (in Peggy's case, literally, since she needs help getting out) in a comfy double recliner.

After settling in, we head downtown to have a snack (having skipped lunch). We find a brewery where we order a couple of delicious, freshly-baked pretzel twists to go along with a beer (for me) and a "5-ounce sampler" for Peggy. The latter, it turns out, consists of *six five-ounce glasses* of a selection of the brewery's beers. Satiated, we stagger from our booth and, with some effort, find our way out the door and onto the street. Too plastered to drive back to the B&B, we check out the town. I, of course, locate a shop which sells paintings, and upon closer inspection find that I am already familiar with the proprietor having met her previously at an art show we frequent in Philadelphia each year. We spend a pleasant half hour there (allowing us to sober up gracefully for the trip back). We return downtown a few hours later for dinner at another brewery, though both of us abstain from the hard stuff this time.

For those of you keeping track and despite the rain, the duct-tape on the bumper seems to be holding the car's undercarriage in place. We are carrying around the rest of the roll just in case, however.

Tomorrow we head up to **Terre Haute, Indiana** where we hope to make it to the **Swope Art Museum**. There are flood warnings for the Wabash River basin which runs by the city but we're assured that we'll be able to arrive non-amphibiously. At worst, the duct tape will be put to the test.

Last Room in the Daze Inn

Day 6 (Saturday, May 28, 2011): Columbia, MO to Terre Haute, IN (285 miles)

We left Columbia after a nice breakfast with a couple from Massachusetts who were also staying at our B&B. Our experience with the student-run bed *and* breakfast was very satisfying, a nice respite in a great college town. We'll come here again sometime.

Checked the duct tape for stability and headed back onto Route 70 toward **Terre Haute**. We have an uneventful drive past farms, farms and more farms. Really getting tired of farms....

A few more hours of farms and we cross the swollen **Wabash River** into Indiana and Terre Haute where we planned to visit the **Swope Art Museum** downtown and stay for the night before proceeding to Indianapolis tomorrow morning. The Swope was founded in the early Forties and the core of its collection is a room full of great Forties paintings. That one room made it worth the visit; there is not much more of great interest, however. The downtown is old and empty, a veritable ghost town (in truth, it is probably more active when **Indiana State University**, just down the block, is in session).

We walk across the street to get ourselves a room at a respectable-looking Hilton Garden Inn. Well, there were no rooms available at the respectable inn. Nor were there rooms at any of the next half-dozen places we called. The **Indianapolis 500** is tomorrow and virtually every hotel room within 75 miles of Indianapolis is booked (full disclosure: it never dawned on me when I originally planned the trip that the 500 occurs on Memorial Day weekend, precisely when we planned on visiting Indianapolis; however, when I did figure it out I at least had the presence of mind to reserve a room for *tomorrow* night in Indy, never dreaming that rooms for tonight would be filled more than an hour's drive away).

After numerous fruitless calls to other hotels, we finally reach the desk clerk at the Terre Haute Days Inn. Says he has "limited rooms" available and puts the receiver down to handle some "business"----for the next twenty-five minutes! We can hear him shooting the bull and we repeatedly scream into the phone hoping he'll remember to deal with us before he gives away the last purportedly "no smoking" room. Losing faith, we drive ten minutes to the motel and walk into the grimy reception area. There behind the desk stands a grizzled old guy looking the part of a serial killer whom I take to be the desk manager, front pocket stuffed with a pack of Marlboros, and a woman with half the normal allotment of teeth. Sheepishly, I tell him I'm still on the phone with him (which he confirms by picking

The Days Inn (above) tripled their rates for the Indy 500. Below, the mighty (swollen) Wabash River.

up his receiver and talking into it, strangely amused to hear himself repeated on my phone). He apologizes for forgetting about us and offers us what is clearly the last room in town.

What a dump! Their $31 rooms (see photo on the previous page) are $94 tonight and since there's no manger to sleep in we accept his offer with trepidation bordering on downright fear. "No smoking" means, I think, that no one has smoked here since this morning. Place smells like an old locker. And don't even ask me about the free wi-fi (you're not getting this by email on Saturday, are you?) or the free hot breakfast (think we'll pass). We even consider doing a wash in the laundry room but decide that the dirty clothes would stay cleaner if we didn't. And wandering around a dirty old motel filled to the brim with tea partier NASCAR types is a disconcerting proposition.

We quickly elect to escape the motel for a few hours in an effort to maintain our equilibrium. We spend an hour eating dinner at an Olive Garden (that's as good as it gets here) and then go to a movie (*Water for Elephants* based on the book we both read and enjoyed).

When we return to the motel the place looks like a Kmart parking lot. At least our duct-taped car looks at home. Our plastic room keys no longer work. We walk around to the reception hole which is now unattended (a "no vacancy" sign has been hastily taped to the door). Luckily, Peggy recognizes the slime-ball desk clerk slinking away and I track him down. He puts down his Marlboro long enough to reprogram our keys, telling us to "have a good night" (I wish!). So now, as I finish this, we sit in the room, wash our hands frequently and look forward to leaving town tomorrow at the crack of dawn. Not looking forward to sleeping on this bowed bed with pillows like sacks of potatoes.

Think we'll skip Terre Haute next time. Hoping tomorrow will be a better day....

Indianapolis is OK by Me

Day 7 (Sunday, May 29, 2011): Terre Haute, IN to Indianapolis, IN (75 miles)

I couldn't sleep much last night. Potato sack pillows are hardly a prescription for comfort. Couldn't get up and out of the Daze Inn fast enough this morning. We were entitled to a free breakfast but couldn't even stomach the concept of eating food emanating from this dump so we headed out to a nearby Cracker Barrel (top of the barrel in Terre Haute).

On the road again, but only for a little while. We couldn't send out yesterday's journal entry using the Daze Inn free wifi (because it was nonfunctional, of course) so we sought out another McDonald's to catch up on our email (we never eat there; we just use their bathrooms and wifi and purchase an occasional $1 ice tea special where available). We motor a quick 75 miles north to the big city—**Indianapolis**. After last night (and never having been to the Big I), we were anxious about what we'd find. Another grimy monument to our grandparents' generation? Hardly. At least in the environs of our downtown Embassy Suites Hotel, the city is glorious. And it's summer (upper 80's) to boot.

We're unique in Indianapolis. The **Indy 500** each year draws about *a quarter MILLION attendees* (half of whom stayed at our motel last night) and this was its 100th anniversary edition. Everyone in the city was there---except us! Maybe we were just brilliant contrarians: what better way to avoid the museum crowds than to plan your Indianapolis museum visits on the day of the 500? Well, we outsmarted 'em. Despite reports of record traffic tie-ups, we didn't experience any traffic at all and the museums were EMPTY! What geniuses we are!

Our first destination was the **Indiana State Museum**, a beautiful (and huge) new facility built along Indianapolis' downtown canal (who knew Indianapolis had canals?) just a short walk from our hotel. In addition to an exhibition of Indiana Oddities (e.g., tree stumps containing Confederate buckshot and a 1957 microwave oven as large as a big-screen TV and as costly, at the time, as a new car), we saw a great private collection of Indiana art from the Thirties and Forties (not just serendipity, as we had planned to visit this one). Next we headed out to the **Indianapolis Museum of Art**, about six miles north. This is truly a world-class museum in a beautiful building sporting a terrific collection. We spent 3 1/2 hours (lunch included) and enjoyed it very much.

We head back to the hotel where we could finally check in. We've gone from the ridiculous (Daze Inn) back to the sublime. Really nice, clean (we don't take that for granted anymore!) and comfortable. No need to keep our suitcases closed to avoid creepy-crawling freeloaders like last night!

It is interesting to note the differences between the better-heeled Indy 500 crowd here and the more dubious Indy fans at the Daze Inn. A different world entirely (though we still couldn't see the attraction in sitting in upper-80's heat to watch stinky cars orbit a track for hours at a time; guess we don't have the requisite attention span).

A good day overall (we were due after yesterday's fiasco) except for the misstep I took entering the hotel (pulled a back muscle, I think). Mobile but will hurt more tomorrow, I'm sure. Perhaps I'll use duct tape...

Tomorrow we sleep late then head to out to finish our Indianapolis museum trifecta with a visit to the Eiteljorg, a museum of western art and Native American culture within walking distance of the hotel. All those Indy 500 fans don't know what they're missing....

A Day in the Country

Day 8 (Monday, May 30, 2011): Indianapolis, IN to Granville, OH (200 miles)

Slept a little later this morning in our luxurious Embassy Suites suite (sweet!). After breakfast we headed over to the **Eiteljorg Museum of American Indians and Western Art** about six blocks from the hotel in downtown Indianapolis. Filled with historical and contemporary art of the American West and Native American art and artifacts, it was a pleasant way to spend a couple of hours. Had to drag Peggy away.

Indianapolis was a wonderful stop, even if we didn't follow the crowds to the Speedway. Much more to see next time we come through (Indianapolis Indians Triple-A baseball maybe?).

We are back on the road again by early afternoon, heading for **Granville, Ohio** (northwest of Columbus) where we booked a small B&B. We stop for lunch and a fill-up near **Springfield, Ohio**. We pass a grimy looking Sunoco which Peggy quickly spots as the obvious gasoline bargain in the area. I long for the clean, streamlined Shell station across the street (with the slightly higher-priced gasoline) but, as usual, I lose. We pull into the Sunoco. What a pit! It is the Days Inn of gas stations. Grease and grime everywhere. Check the photo on the following page and you'll see that the gas pump we used *was held together with duct tape!* Poetic justice, I guess. If it works for Sunoco it should continue to work for us.

Duct-taped gas pump at the Days Inn of gas stations near Springfield, Ohio

We arrive, intact, at the **Orchard House Bed & Breakfast** at around 5 PM. Recently opened, it is run by a couple of young guys recently relocated from Washington, DC. One worked as a speechwriter in the Obama administration, the other continues to consult for a major international consulting company. The place has cats, dogs, rabbits, ducks, chickens, llamas and other assorted wildlife on about a dozen acres. I keep my distance but Peg takes a look. The animals serve more as pets than livestock, so I'm not sure how this operation translates economically, but that's not our problem. The house is a mid-19th century Greek revival, nicely redone.

After check-in we head to the nearby town center of Granville, home of **Denison University**. What a treat! This is a picture-perfect midwestern gem of a town, with a tree-lined Main Street flanked by gorgeous 19th century homes in pristine condition. Picturesque churches sit on all four corners of the town's main intersection. We have a nice dinner at a brew house and stroll through a portion of the college campus. We then walk over to the town green where the entire community is on hand for a free Memorial Day concert by a British Invasion cover band (mostly Beatles tunes). It is 95 degrees today, but we don't care. It's a really nice way to complete the evening. (And to top things off, the Red Sox are on TV when we get back to the inn. What could be better? Well, they could have won, I suppose.)

One funny coincidence. Although our lodging is situated in a rural area probably 40 minutes from Columbus, there are several small corporate headquarters nearby. The one *directly* across the road is Paramount Financial Group, a real estate syndication company which was (and may still be) a client of my old law firm (in my own practice area). Small world.

Tomorrow we can look forward to a nice breakfast here at our inn followed by a four-hour drive into southwestern Pennsylvania where we have reservations to tour Frank Lloyd Wright's **Fallingwater** and will stay at another country inn. Stay tuned.

Orchard House B&B, built in the 1850s

Our room was in the main house, fortunately

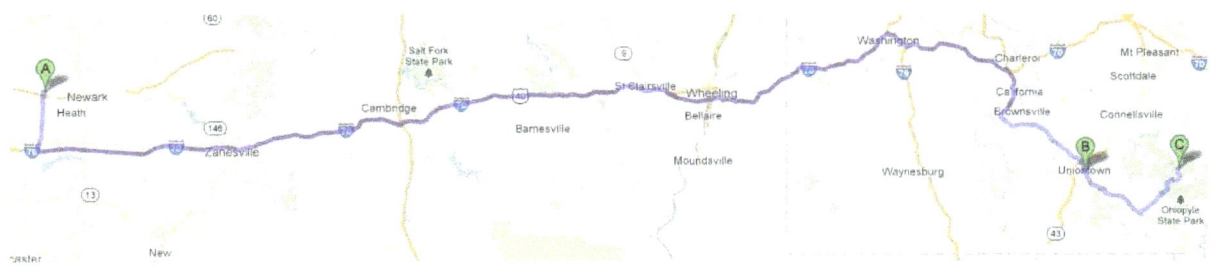

Half-Cooked in Uniontown

Day 9 (Tuesday, May 31, 2011): Granville, OH to Uniontown, PA (230 miles)

We enjoyed an excellent breakfast at our Granville bed and breakfast and then hit the road. Our plan for this, our ninth (ugh!) day on the road was to visit **Fallingwater**, Frank Lloyd Wright's residential masterpiece, and then head to nearby **Uniontown, Pennsylvania** to a bed and breakfast.

Our trip east across I-70 was uneventful, though the countryside in southeastern Ohio was rolling and pretty. When we left the interstate, travel was slower and more tortuous. The detour to Fallingwater took us through several old coal mining towns whose better days are behind them, then up and down a series of winding mountain roads in southwestern Pennsylvania (about an hour and a half from Pittsburgh). When we finally reached Fallingwater, we grabbed a quick lunch and took an hour-long guided tour of the house and grounds. As the photo on the following page indicates, it is rather amazing. The house is a marvel of engineering featuring cantilevered construction which allows substantial portions of the residence to hover beside and above a dramatic waterfall and stream in the midst of about 7,000 acres of forest. While Wright was a cantankerous old fart with many faults, he did have a "can-do" attitude and achieved, at least in this case, remarkable results. The home was built in the late Thirties as a weekend getaway for a Pittsburgh retail magnate and his family and is preserved just as the family left it upon the death of their adult son (the end of the family line). So its

A luscious view of Fallingwater, Frank Lloyd Wright's residential masterpiece set deep in the woods near Mill Run, Pennsylvania

furnishings and art, including two great Diego Riveras and some fine Southwestern pottery, remain in place. Built primarily of stone quarried on the property, the rooms were reasonably cool despite the high 80's temperatures this afternoon. They charge a steep $20 per person to tour the property and it is a challenge to get there but we both considered it time and money well spent (as contrasted with tonight's dinner experience).

After Fallingwater, we drove another twenty winding miles to a bed and breakfast we'd chosen in **Uniontown, Pennsylvania**. While the B&B is nice, it is relatively large and its hosts seemed underwhelmed by our presence. Either they've been running a B&B too long or we've been on the road too long (or both). There is nothing really to do here so we walked part of the grounds, searching for the proverbial needle in the haystack (see photos). We didn't find it.

The farm girl...

and the farm guy at the bed & breakfast in Uniontown

Our entertainment for the evening was dinner. Getting tired of the same old same old, we elected to sample an Asian restaurant with an appealing menu. We arrived at 6:10. There was one large party in the restaurant but only one or two other couples when we came in. Things slid downhill faster than a fumbled chopstick. The air conditioning was virtually non-existent, FoxNews (dis)graced the TV and our harried waitress was apoplectically apologetic about her pathetically slow service. As the evening dragged on, the apologies multiplied. We were calm and understanding (primarily since we had nothing else to do). We had been waiting for our entrée for about an hour when the power outage occurred. A blown fuse--- theirs, not mine (at least not yet). We just sat there in the dark, keeping our (relative) cool. The good news was that the outage silenced the bad news from FoxNews; the worse news was that (supposedly) our entrée had been half-cooked when the power failed so it would need to be redone (that excuse itself was half-cooked.) Getting a little more annoyed now. The power returned in about ten minutes and another 25 passed without our damn entrée. How long does it take to cook a few shrimp? Everyone who came in after us had already been served. Our waitress set personal and house apology records. Not to worry, we were told, we'd get a discount for our patience. The food finally arrives at 7:40 (an hour and a half after we arrived). Edible but nothing to write home about (though, remarkably, I'm doing just that). It could probably have been prepared in five minutes. More apologies (setting the records now for Uniontown and all of southwestern Pennsylvania). We eat (that took about 3 minutes) and get the bill. They take off a whopping $3 as a courtesy discount. Big whoop! On our way out, the owner asks about our experience and we tell him. He apologizes (probably his own personal record) but instead of a larger discount he offers us a gift certificate for the next time we come by. That'll be the day....

Uniontown officially joins Terre Haute as a destination to be avoided at all cost.

Tomorrow we drive to Halifax, Pennsylvania, near Harrisburg, for an evening with Peggy's aunt and uncle. Home cooked food. Yesssss!

And yes, the duct tape is still holding.

Aunt Carol, Uncle Herb and the C.I.A.

Days 10 & 11 (Wednesday/Thursday, June 1-2, 2011): Uniontown, PA to Halifax, PA (225 miles) and Halifax, PA to Poughkeepsie, NY (230 miles)

Keeping ourselves consistently a day or two behind the tornadoes (this time a rare but deadly event in Springfield, MA, through which we'll pass tomorrow), we departed Uniontown in the coal country of southwestern Pennsylvania on Wednesday morning and headed east to **Halifax, Pennsylvania**, a small hamlet above the Susquehanna River in the mountains north of **Harrisburg**. Once again, we scale a series of tortuous mountain roads (with occasionally disarming hairpin turns) to spend the evening with Peggy's Aunt Carol and Uncle Herb for our first truly hosted night on the cross-country trek. The home they built for themselves in retirement a dozen years ago is gracious and sited beautifully amid gardens, forests and rolling farmland. Though isolated, this is inspiring country, as nice as any we've seen on our seemingly endless journey. We enjoyed good conversation and a nice, home-cooked meal for the first time in nearly two weeks. A welcome change!

This morning, after bidding our adieus, we headed back down the mountain to make our way north through **Scranton, Pennsylvania**, the **Pocono Mountains** and into the **Hudson River Valley** north of New York City. A few random observations about Pennsylvania: (1) it's huge, (2) it is way more beautiful than we give it credit for and (3) it has more work zones than you can shake a stick at, both on the interstates and on the lonely two-lane country roads. We weren't five minutes into today's trip when we were stopped by one of those ubiquitous, neon-

A downtown somewhere near Halifax, Pennsylvania

Homes for the upper crust of the aviary world

clad road crew members flipping his STOP sign in our face as we awaited the clearance of largely phantom traffic from the single lane ahead. These guys are constantly babbling on their walkie-talkies, ostensibly to ascertain the presence or absence of traffic or (more probably) ordering lunch. Perhaps the oncoming traffic was, in fact, delivering lunch...

Speaking of lunch, today's stop was at the **Apple Valley Restaurant** in the Pocono Mountain resort community of **Milford, Pennsylvania**. It was listed in the AAA guide, which gave me pause to begin with. From the looks of it, it was a survivor from the Fifties and Sixties, when people last flocked to the Poconos. It gave me further pause when a gaggle of seriously senior citizens emerged from the restaurant with that satisfied (but slightly gassy) look on their faces, but since both of us had to pee very badly (compliments of those jumbo $1 iced teas from McDonald's), we bolted in. Inside, the patrons were similarly superannuated, making us feel like teenagers. And, in the end, the food was adequate (for those customers who still had teeth to chew it).

Uncle Herb, Aunt Carol and Peggy.

We reached the Hudson River Valley by mid-afternoon and made our way to the **FDR House and Library** in **Hyde Park, New York**. We took a tour of his humongous home (elegant in an early twentieth century way but preppy, dark and dingy to us; see photograph below) and his presidential library, which had a mountain of exhibits relating to all aspects of his life and public career. An interesting visit, though we were somewhat rushed as it was nearing closing time.

Our next brilliant idea was to visit Hyde Park's other claim to fame, the **Culinary Institute of America**, to experience dinner in one of their five student-staffed training restaurants. Expecting it to be a modest facility, we were surprised to discover that the CIA is actually an enormous modern campus spread over acres and acres along the banks of the Hudson River. We arrived for our 6:00 reservation with just enough time to park the car, extract some more presentable clothes from the trunk and change furtively in the passenger seat hoping to avoid an audience. So, how did we rank the Culinary Institute's dinner against last

The modest little house of Franklin D. Roosevelt in Hyde Park, New York.

evening's home-cooked meal? Here's the blow-by-blow rundown:

Ambience: the CIA restaurant was large and well-decorated (the one we chose was an Italian restaurant), but impersonal. Aunt Carol and Uncle Herb's dining room was cozy and filled with character. *ADVANTAGE:* Aunt Carol and Uncle Herb.

Ordering Process: at the CIA we needed to ask what "spec" was (some overpriced cut of ham), what "mache" was (some overpriced version of arugula), how much the 18-year old scotch cost (too much) and whether the Italian beer selection was light or dark (our student waiter had no clue but could disappear into the bowels of the restaurant and fetch us an answer if we cared enough to wait). At Aunt Carol and Uncle Herb's, our hosts divined our needs and prepared us chicken, simple as that. *ADVANTAGE:* Aunt Carol and Uncle Herb.

Food Quality and Value: at the CIA we ordered a pork tenderloin (Peggy) and a swordfish dish (Art). Both were just okay, no way justifying their $22-24 prices. Aunt Carol cooked really decent chicken and didn't charge us a nickel. *ADVANTAGE:* Aunt Carol and Uncle Herb.

Dessert Course: the CIA offered a warm chocolate cake with strawberry sauce. Not bad, but it took almost as long as the shrimp we ordered in the God-forsaken Asian restaurant from a couple of nights ago. The waiter's excuse was equally unsatisfying ("it got busy" or something like that). In fact, while we were waiting, a waiter tried to serve us bread again. Could the waitress at the Asian restaurant have been a CIA graduate? Hmmm... Well, Aunt Carol prepared strawberry shortcake which came out in a flash and tasted just fine, thanks. *ADVANTAGE:* Aunt Carol and Uncle Herb.

Personality: the CIA waiter was young and geeky. Aunt Carol and Uncle Herb are fun family. *ADVANTAGE:* Aunt Carol and Uncle Herb.

Summary: If you need a summary, you haven't been paying attention.

Sleeping this off tonight in another Holiday Inn Express, last one, I hope, for a while. Tomorrow, we head for home, about a 3 1/2-hour ride. Let's rev up the Duct-Tape Mobile and get ourselves home!

Duct Tape Denouement

Day 12 (Friday, June 3, 2011): Poughkeepsie, NY to Natick, MA (190 miles)

Well, you don't have to read any more of my cross-country ruminations. We are finally home. We spent last night in **Poughkeepsie, New York** and drove up the **Taconic State Parkway** (a classic and very lovely old-style parkway running up eastern New York State) through the **Berkshires** and across the Mass Pike, arriving home in Natick, Massachusetts by noontime.

Since our auto mechanic is located half a block away, we ran by there shortly after our return to let him witness our duct tape mastery. He seemed rather unimpressed, removing all of my overlapping tape and replacing it with just a couple well-placed strips pending the arrival of a replacement for the damaged undercarriage. In fairness, he did have the advantage of being able to raise the car to a height of five feet rather than crawling beneath it like I did.

So far, things back home seem to be in good order, though the battery charger which was left on our '96 Acura (parked in our garage level here) had been inadvertently (?) disconnected, allowing the battery to die. The car is also covered with a thick layer of dust and grime. Yuch! I'll deal with that tomorrow....

Weather is gorgeous here, around 70 degrees and dry. Hope it continues. It was a fun trip, but it is good to be finally home.

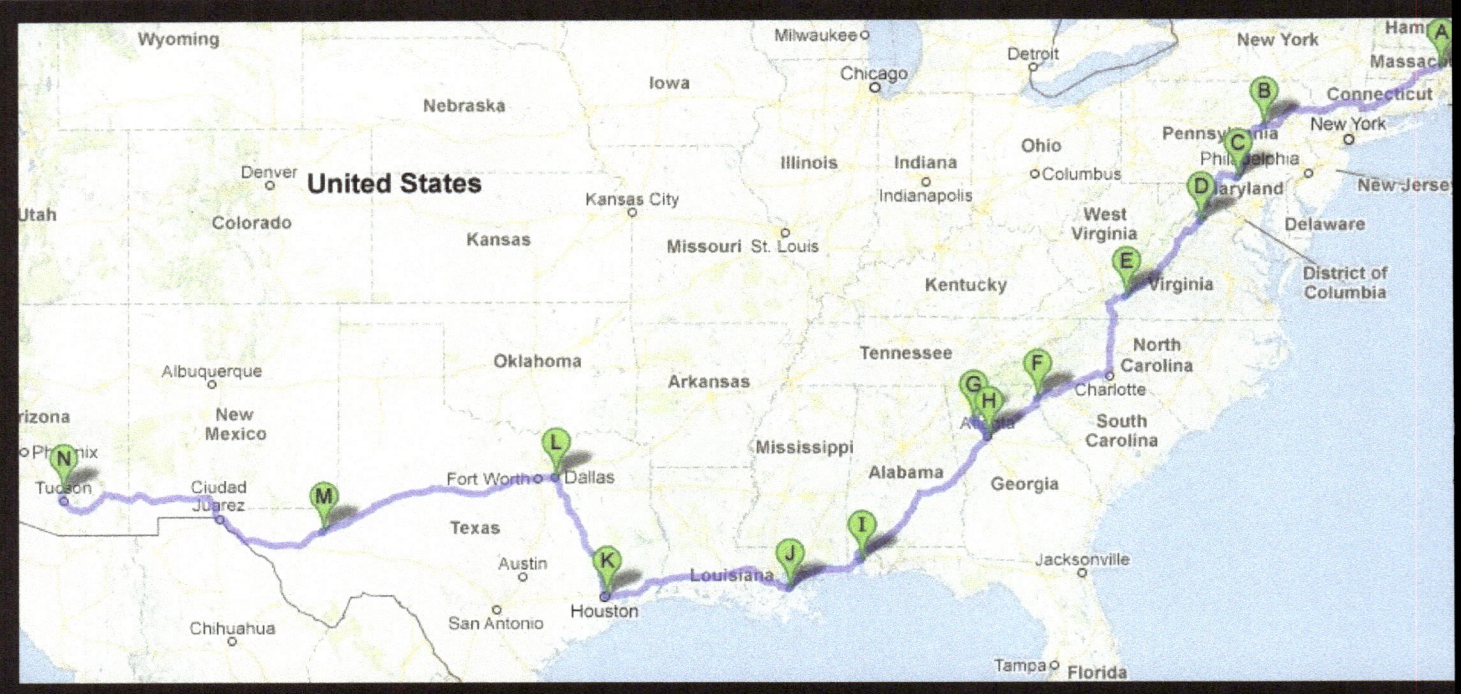

Trip Two

God, Guns and the Rump at the Pump

Natick, Massachusetts to Oro Valley (Tucson), Arizona
11 Days, 3,264 Miles
October 24-November 3, 2011

The Electric Cow Paddy

Days 1 & 2 (Monday/Tuesday, October 24-25, 2011): Natick, MA to Bloomsburg, PA (336 miles) and Bloomsburg, PA to Stephens City, VA (210 miles)

Well, friends, whether you like it or not, you're on the receiving end of my latest cross-country journal, chronicling the noteworthy, peculiar or just plain mundane trivia which catches my fancy as we motor our way from Natick, Massachusetts to Tucson, Arizona. I wasn't planning on writing a blog this time but Peggy insisted that some of you have such boring lives that you actually enjoyed my "Duct Tape Diaries" drivel the last time we traversed this great land.

Peggy and I left Natick on Monday morning, making it to **Bloomsburg, Pennsylvania**, the home (who knew?) of **Bloomsburg University**. Wikipedia lists among its prominent alumni the immortal Joe Colone (who played pro basketball for the New York Knicks for one year, in 1948-49). Oh, that Bloomburg! Notwithstanding its lack of notoriety, it is a pretty town with a nice country inn (**The Inn at Turkey Hill**). An oasis located behind a busy intersection right off the interstate, it was actually a nice place to stay. Its restaurant is reputedly a gem, with entrees breaking the $40 barrier (that's a heckuva lot for Bloomsburg). Since it was Peggy's --th birthday (hint: there's a Beatles' song about that age), we partook of a nice meal (sharing a halibut, some fried green tomatoes and a heartier-than-necessary dessert). And since it was her birthday, I let Peggy watch the World Series.

We headed south on Tuesday morning, forsaking the interstate for a little more local color. The foliage was fading but still impressive as we wound our way across mountain passes bound for a stop at **Gettysburg, Pennsylvania**. There we checked out the Civil War battlefield visitor center and museum. I visited this battlefield once before, in 1962, when my Pony League all-star baseball team (I was there for my glove, not my bat, and because our team needed at least one representative) went to nearby **Hagerstown, Maryland** for a tournament (my history teacher was a coach and I also recall my naïve surprise at the fact that the couple of black players on our team couldn't stay with the rest of us but were farmed out to local black families willing to accommodate them). We watched a movie describing the gruesome battle (a good overview except that the actor

Multiple cow butts tend to produce...

...a plethora of cow poop and...

...as Peggy's visage can attest, a pungent odor

A hint of the transmission station over the hill

The Inn at Vauclause Spring in Stephens City, Virginia. Once home of the artist John Chumley, it is now a bed-and-breakfast

reading Lincoln's lines made him sound like a twit) and then viewed the rather amazing **Gettysburg Cyclorama**, a painting-in-the-round originally done by a French artist in 1883 and recently restored and reinstalled in a new building at the visitor center. It is 27 feet high and 359 feet in circumference. Following a dose of history, we headed into town for some lunch. Eschewing the obvious tourist traps, we found an old diner whose waitresses (with just a couple of exceptions) were even older than your typical Walmart greeters. The "younger" ones (by comparison only, not in an absolute sense, to be sure) seemed to have cornered the local market on eye mascara.

We completed Tuesday's journey by travelling another hundred or so miles further south through southern Pennsylvania and across slivers of Maryland and West Virginia and into the luscious **Shenandoah Valley** of northwestern Virginia. As I write this, we are holed up at the **Inn at Vauclause Spring** in **Stephens City, Virginia**. Amazingly, we have been here before: before it was even an inn! Somewhere around thirty years ago we came to this very place to visit the then owner of this historic homestead, the artist **John Chumley** (1928-1984). We came to meet the artist because we were considering the purchase of an earlier work he had done (in the 1950s) of two young boys "crawfishing" in a local stream. Chumley painted in the Wyeth tradition and was a charming man whom we very much enjoyed meeting. Some of his works are displayed here. (We did buy the painting—it was a lot of money for us especially in those days—but had to sell it a year or two later to complete the down payment needed to purchase our first (or maybe second, we can't remember) house.)

So with fond memories, we came here hoping to rekindle the idyllic feeling of that first visit. We're staying in an outbuilding (by which I *don't* mean "outhouse") which is essentially a log cabin with character. They have 103 acres here so, after checking in, we headed off for a walk. We had been directed to a "cow path" which led up a pretty hill. A little less idyllic than I recall, however, as we dodged prodigious cow turds until we scaled the hill and saw the massive electric transmission facility on the other side. You could actually *hear* the power pulsing through the overhead lines! I half-expected the cows we encountered to be sporting dual heads, but as I could only see their butts I couldn't tell (unless, of course, they had butts at both ends which would have explained the plethora of poop).

Oh, well, off to bed (there's no TV and thank God no World Series game tonight). We'll email this tomorrow at the first McDonald's we find (since there's no wi-fi here either except in a two square foot area in the main house which they say has a "spotty" connection).

Two Toilets and Three Art Museums

Days 3 through 6 (Wednesday/Saturday, October 26-29, 2011): Stephens City, VA to Christiansburg, Virginia (205 miles), and on to Seneca, SC (306 miles including detour to Asheville, NC), Atlanta, GA (185 miles including detour to Cartersville, GA) and Mobile, AL (329 miles)

Well, it's been four days and about a thousand miles since my first update (and my last confession). Here's the scoop on our comings and goings since.

When we last communicated we were fluorescing from the high voltage power lines which permeated the **Inn at Vauclause Spring** in **Stephens City, Virginia**. After a nice breakfast in the main house, we departed for the nearby town of **Front Royal, Virginia** where we entered **Shenandoah National Park** via the picturesque **Skyline Drive** which winds southward through the mountains. The views were breathtaking and the fall colors only slightly beyond peak. We drove up and down, left and right, twisting and turning at a breakneck 35 mph until, at about the 60-mile mark (almost two hours), I was bordering on nausea and more than ready to battle the big rigs along Interstate 81 instead. By late afternoon, we checked in at the **Oaks Victorian Inn** in **Christiansburg, Virginia**. Ironically, it is run by a Jewish couple from New Jersey (undoubtedly the only two Jews in Christiansburg). Our room was elegant and well-equipped (perhaps *over*-equipped). I began to worry that we, like the cows back in Stephens City, had each grown two

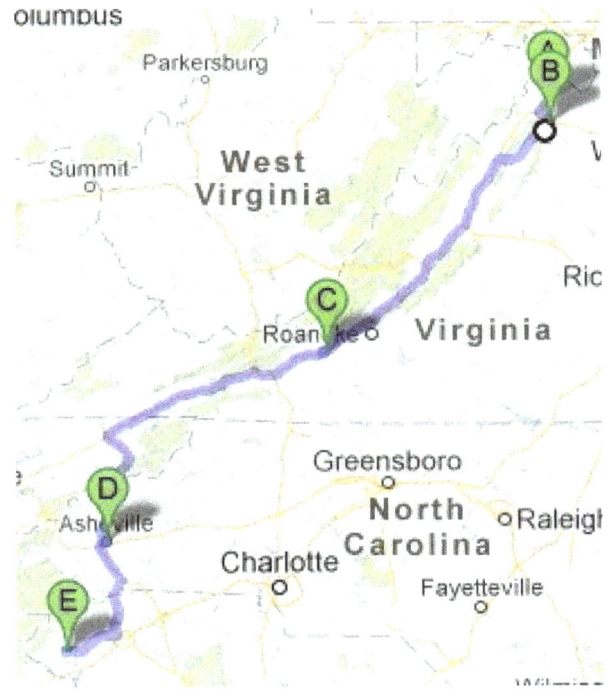

A restored commercial building in the business district of Christiansburg, Virginia

A view from Skyline Drive in Shenandoah National Park

An example of the many sophisticated crafts on display in the galleries of Asheville, NC

A painting by Douglas Gorsline, from the mid-1940s, in the Mobile Museum of Art

butts from our high-voltage exposure since our room had an enormous bathroom with bathtub, shower and, rather astoundingly, *two* separate toilets. Actually kind of useful in the after-breakfast rush…

On Thursday we headed out from Christiansburg toward **Asheville, North Carolina**, where we stopped for lunch at a funky new Spanish tapas restaurant (very good!) before checking out a half-dozen arts and crafts galleries and hitting our first art museum of the trip. Asheville is a very worthwhile destination deserving of more than a lunch stop. From Asheville we travelled another couple of hours south to **Seneca, South Carolina** (a "suburb" of Clemson) where we dined and spent the evening with old friends from our days in Cambridge, Massachusetts.

Friday was our Georgia day. Our first stop was in **Cartersville, Georgia** (about 25 miles northwest of Atlanta) where we visited the **Booth Western Art Museum**. The cavernous (120,000 square feet), eight-year-old museum houses

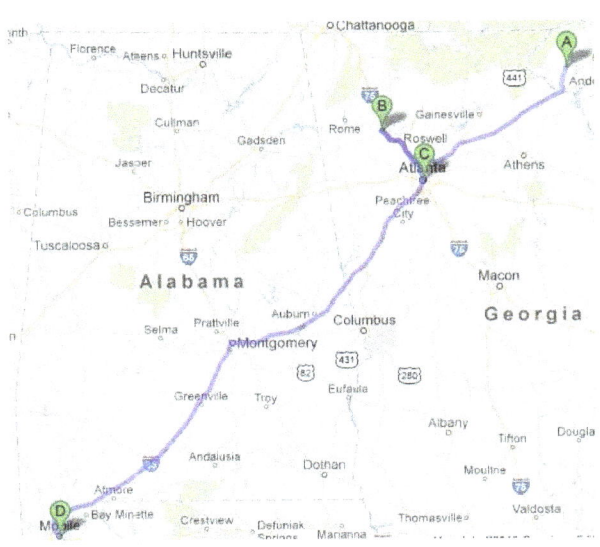

the largest permanent exhibition space for Western art (i.e., art of the American west) in the country. No idea whatsoever why it is located in Cartersville, Georgia, but it is a spectacular venue with a great collection. We returned to **Atlanta** to spend the evening with another wonderful couple whom we've known for over 30 years.

Tonight, I write this from a very elegant, newly restored antebellum mansion in the historic downtown of **Mobile, Alabama**. It is the centerpiece of a couple of blocks which were purchased by a New York preservationist who has or is in the process of restoring each of its

The newly-restored Fort Conde Inn in Mobile, Alabama

thirteen original 19th-century residential buildings. The building in which we are staying was originally constructed in 1836, making it the second-oldest home in Mobile. The restoration was completed just a few months ago and the place is now the **Fort Conde Inn**, a luxury boutique hotel. Using the poor-traveller-passing-through-last-minute-inquiry technique, we were able to negotiate a sizzling 20% discount.

Upon our arrival in Mobile, we scored our third art museum in three days, the aptly named **Mobile Museum of Art**, where we pretty much had the entire museum to ourselves (not surprising on a football Saturday in the South). Ho-hum collection until we noticed an entire section devoted exclusively to the 1930s-1940s American art we love, including major works by two of the artists in our collection. They also had a wonderful Smithsonian Travelling exhibition of photographs taken of Elvis Presley during his inaugural national tour in 1956. Actually quite fascinating.

Tomorrow we're off to New Orleans (where, like Mobile, we've never been). Should be fun.

To our friends and family in New England: enjoy the snow! I'm sure you wouldn't want to endure the oppressive seventy-degree heat we're expecting tomorrow. Ha ha ha....

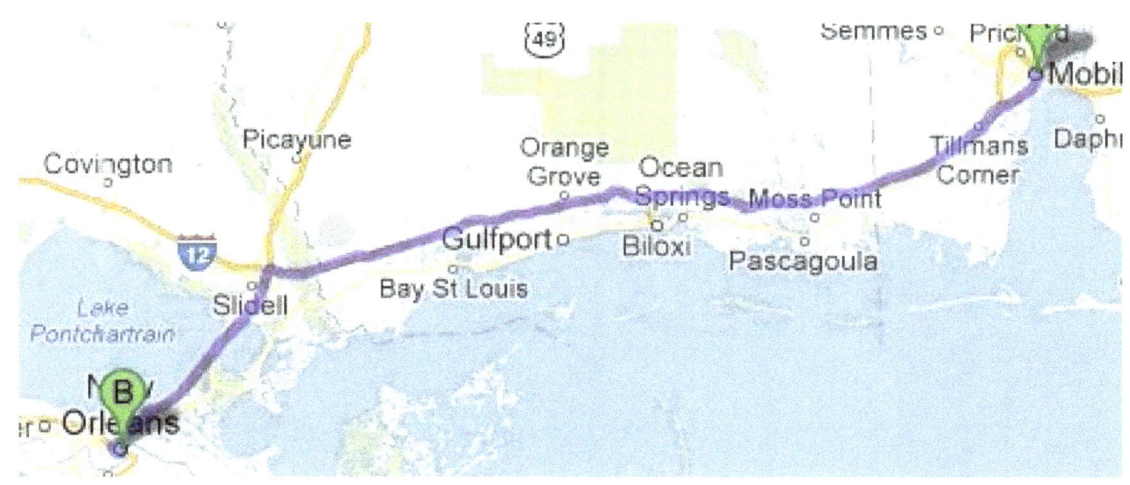

Guns, Jesus and the "Big Easy"

Day 7 (Sunday, October 30, 2011): Mobile, AL to New Orleans, LA (146 miles)

It's Sunday so this must be N'awlunz (**New Orleans** for those of you unfamiliar with the local drawl). We arrived here following an uneventful two-hour ride from Mobile. Highlight of the morning was filling up the gas tank at less than $3.14 per gallon just outside of Mobile--not surprising somehow since the city smells like a refinery when the wind is right.

Since we're indisputably in the Deep South (and were bored on our trip to The Big Easy), we decided (at the suggestion of one of our dedicated readers) to pit guns against Jesus by counting the roadside billboards touting one or the other and keeping score. A small sample so far but guns are burying Jesus (so to speak) two to one. But Jesus was able to boast at least two roadside mega-churches (though a majority of the parishioners were probably packing heat). More reports on this competition as we enter Governor Rick Perry's domain tomorrow.

Upon our arrival in The Crescent City (the first visit for both of us), we parked the car in the hotel lot and hopped the trolley downtown. We began on **Bourbon Street** with lunch at **The Red Fish Grill**, consuming a pair of Abita Turbodogs (a particularly drinkable Louisiana dark beer) and splitting a cup of alligator gumbo, a blackened catfish sandwich and a double-chocolate bread pudding which was disgustingly delicious. Ugh. Suffice it to say that we've been unable to contemplate eating since.

Bourbon Street in New Orleans

Bourbon Street is a little like Las Vegas: you need to do it once but that may be enough. Peggy was a bit surprised by its sleaziness. Maybe it was the naked guy dancing on the bar at one of the establishments we passed. The overall scene (naked guy excluded) reminded me of Sunday afternoons at the fraternity house: the look of dissipation on everyone's face and the pervasive odor of stale beer (or worse). We had hoped to catch some afternoon jazz at **Preservation Hall** but it was closed down until the evening. We walked back along **Royal Street** (home of dozens of antiques shops) but (naturally) everything was closed on Sunday.

On the way back to our Garden District hotel we meandered along some side streets gawking at the charming old houses with their elegant columns, sultry porches and fabulous ornamental ironwork. We also peeked into one of New Orleans' legendary cemeteries. A veritable city of crypts, it too was closed on Sunday though I suspect it will be hopping tomorrow night on Halloween.

Tomorrow we begin our endless descent into Texas, home of Dubbya and those loser Rangers. With stops in Houston, Dallas and yet-to-be-determined God-forsaken outposts in West Texas, it will take us at least four days to make it through. Don't hold your breath...

Hitching a ride on the trolley along Magazine Street

A full service law firm, New Orleans style

Double chocolate bread pudding at The Red Fish Grill on Bourbon Street

An impromptu concert

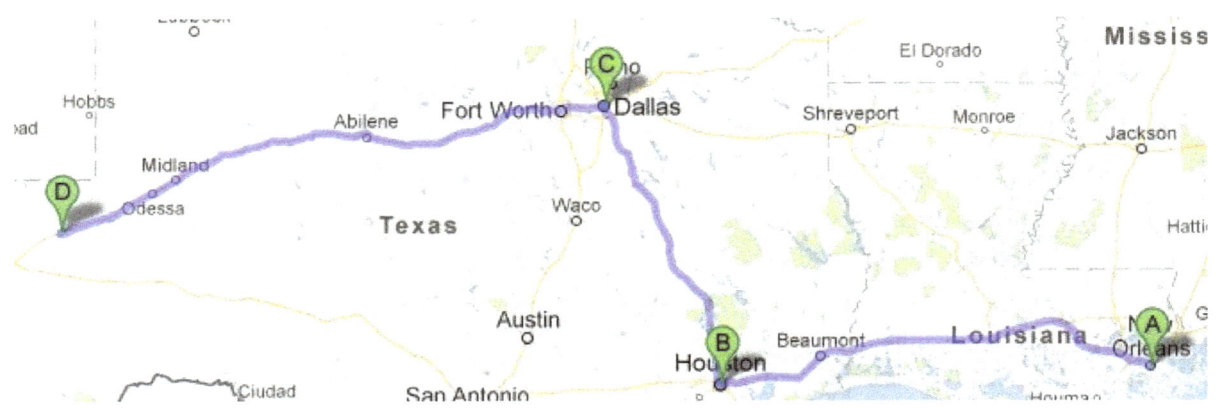

Dust, Duct Tape, Temptation, God and Guns

Days 8 through 10 (Monday/Wednesday, October 31 - November 2, 2011): New Orleans, LA to Houston, TX (348 miles), and on to Dallas, TX (239 miles) and Pecos, TX (427 miles)

Just finished showering the dust off my weary body in our hotel room in **Pecos, Texas**. It's been a long driving day, but more about that later.

We left New Orleans on Monday morning, traversing deltas and bayous on our way to visit friends in **Houston** (former neighbors in Natick, Massachusetts). We passed **Minute Maid Park** (where the Astros sucked all summer) before arriving at our friends' new home in a lovely portion of town near **Rice University** (where the husband recently took a job as Dean of Engineering). Before our departure the next morning, we took a quick auto tour of Rice's graceful century-old campus which is situated near Houston's museum district and its medical hub (there are some 40+ impressive hospitals and other medical facilities concentrated within this particular area of the city). The local roads, though, are decidedly unimpressive. Heaving and crumbling roads quite nearly led to a heaving and crumbling Art as I teetered along in the back seat during the thirty-minute tour. Great to see the city but even Costa Rica has better local roadways.

Yesterday, we headed north to visit another pair of friends in **Dallas**. It took nearly 40 miles to escape Houston's endless sprawl after which there was virtually nothing to see the rest of the way to Dallas. The only exception was a 67-foot statue of **Sam Houston** inexplicably appearing alongside the highway outside of

Rice University, Houston, Texas

Huntsville, Texas. Looked like an albino hitchhiker on steroids (like almost everything else in Texas).

Another pleasant visit with friends gave way to another day on the road. We allotted three days to cover the 950 miles between Dallas and Tucson. So with no firm target for the first day's ride, we headed southwest across the endless expanse that is Texas. Today's ride was relatively uneventful until the afternoon when strong wind gusts wreaked havoc on the flat plains and recently plowed fields along the highway. The resultant dust clouds reduced visibility dramatically, sometimes to only a hundred feet or so (particularly challenging if you're travelling anywhere near the posted speed limit of 80). These conditions persisted most of the afternoon, making travel hazardous. I shudder to think how much dust (and fertilizer) we (and our car's air filter) ingested. This, combined with the pervasive smell of petroleum, made for a less than idyllic day's journey.

Speaking of our vehicle, we again found occasion to make judicious use of the roll of duct tape that we stowed in preparation for our cross-country journey. Another strip of plastic came loose (along the cutout for the passenger side rear wheel). Once again, duct tape did the trick (as attested to by the photo on the following page)!

Continuing our effort to expose great art museums in the most unlikely of places, we stopped in **Midland, Texas** (former home to both George Bushes). We checked out the **Museum of the Southwest**, situated rather inauspiciously on a

Duct tape to the rescue, again!

dusty side street in Midland. There were a grand total of two other cars in the parking lot when we arrived (and when we left). We found no attendant or receptionist on duty when we entered, though someone eventually emerged in a coughing fit from a back room to inform us that just one small room was currently open to visitors. But what a room it was! Filled with about fifteen paintings executed in the Twenties, Thirties and Forties by founding members of the Taos Society of Artists, it was part of a gift to the museum by a wealthy oil family of Midland. It was stunning (and nuts) to me to realize that this unattended room contained perhaps $2 million in easily transportable art. On a table in the center of the room was an unsecured copy of the leading study on the Taos Society artists, an out-of-print book which generally sells for about $400. It seemed like a perfect opportunity to enrich our collection and our library at the same time; I don't think anyone would have noticed for days (if at all). But good sense prevailed over temptation and we left everything where we found it. And if any of that cache disappears in the days to come, you are all suspects.

Deciding that any town that suckled George Bush was a poor choice for the Hittners, we headed further on down the road to **Odessa** (like Midland, a smelly petroleum town) in search of a hotel. Amazingly, there was no room at its inns: the town was full! No one had any explanation, but since the Bushes lived in Odessa for a while as well, we decided we were too liberal to sleep there anyway. Of course the three men from Halliburton coming out of the Hampton Inn in orange suits (I kid you not!) gave us more than a little pause. So we hit the road again, travelling another dusty hour or so to the bustling burb of **Pecos,**

The bane of West Texas: a smog-shrouded refinery

Texas, where we found a Holiday Inn Express which would admit anyone, even northeastern liberals. We checked in, then moseyed on down the road to **Alfredo's Mexican Restaurant** for dinner. Talk about a square Peg in a round hole: we were about the only sedan (i.e., non-pickup) in the parking lot and the only ones without dirty blue jeans, overalls and/or cowboy hats and boots. Fortunately, they didn't inquire about our politics and we left well fed (and alive). We returned to our hoppin' Holiday Inn room to rinse off the day's accumulated dust and rest up for another day working our way through the inexhaustible plains of West Texas.

Almost forgot: God (and son Jesus) have nudged into the lead over the gun lobby in the Southern billboard tally by a margin of nine to seven. Although we didn't tally them, I am compelled to observe that the number of billboards touting adult superstores and "gentlemen's" clubs easily exceeded both God and Guns combined. Not at all sure what that means.

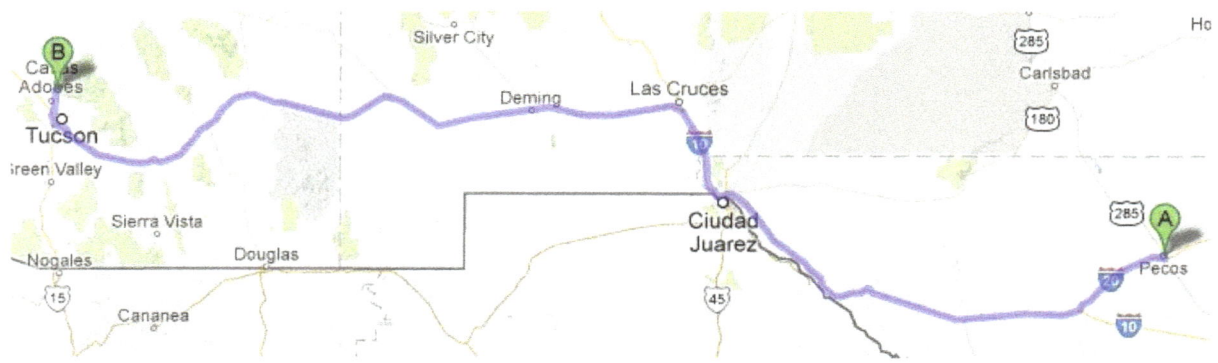

Rump at the Pump

Day 11 (Thursday, November 3, 2011): Pecos, TX to Oro Valley, AZ (530 miles)

Almost too exhausted to write this. We arrived in Tucson today, a day earlier than planned, after a 530-mile drive from West Texas. Soooo glad to be out of there!

We showered in our room at the Pecos Holiday Inn Express before heading downstairs for their free breakfast buffet. The water was such that you couldn't seem to wash the soap off: it was either exceedingly "soft" water or honest-to-God petroleum residue (which, incidentally, was what breakfast tasted like).

Speaking of God, I'm sure you're all breathless for the final tally. Well, the Lord has prevailed, beating the guns into plowshares by a 10 to 7 margin. All's well with the world (assuming, once again, that you don't pit God ads against sex ads, as discussed yesterday, in which case the world is actually pretty screwed up).

We hadn't planned on driving all the way home today but we got off to an early start. Also, we had forgotten that we would gain not one but *two* hours along the way (switching from CDT to MDT and then losing another hour when we entered Arizona which is too backward to adopt Daylight Savings Time). So every three or so hours we drove we gained an hour, meaning it was always too early to stop

Run down gas pump in Deming, New Mexico where someone needed "Help" keeping his pants up

driving. So we didn't.

We passed part of the time listening to an audiobook given us by our Atlanta friends: *Tulia* by Nate Blakeslee. It is the true story about a gross miscarriage of justice perpetrated on a group of mostly black defendants by redneck policemen, prosecutors and judges in the same part of West Texas that we had been traversing. It certainly motivated us to drive faster, but not so fast as to invite attention of any of the local police officers.

Not much of interest to report on the drive home. The only incident of note occurred on a gas stop in **Deming, New Mexico**. Always on the lookout for the cheapest possible gasoline, Peggy directed me to a dilapidated service station on the outskirts of town. While the gas pumps were automated (barely), they were in dire need of an upgrade. In the above photo you'll see what I mean. When offered a receipt, I was prompted to respond "Yes" or "No". The blue buttons in the photo, I believe, represent those two choices though your guess is as good as mine as to which is which. Didn't matter, of course, since no receipt was forthcoming anyway. And to complete the experience, a homeless guy (or perhaps the station owner?) bent down over to the trash bin adjacent to the pump whereupon his pants fell to his knees. From the looks of it, I can only conclude that he was seeking his missing underwear.

Well, we're home at last and happy to be here. Hope you enjoyed these occasional blogs from the real America. Keep in touch.

Trip Three

Take the Long Way Home

**Oro Valley (Tucson), Arizona to Natick, Massachusetts
15 Days, 3,950 Miles
May 21-June 4, 2012**

Who knew Martians abhor train noise?   *Anyone up for an old-fashioned decapitation?*

On the Road Again!

Day 1 (Monday, May 21, 2012): Oro Valley, AZ to Flagstaff, AZ (258 miles)

It's that time of the year again! Peggy and Art have saddled up the old duct-taped Lexus and begun our sixth cross-country jaunt in three years. And you get to read all about it in far more detail than is either reasonable or healthy.

I write this from atop our Tempur-Pedic mattress (our first such experience; will report on it tomorrow) in a bed-and-breakfast inaptly called the **England House** in **Flagstaff, Arizona**, where we are mentally preparing for our virgin viewing of the **Grand Canyon** tomorrow morning. Three winters in Arizona and we've yet to see the Humongous Hole. More on that to follow....

Our first day on the road back was uneventful but hotter than hell. As in a sizzling 108 degrees! By the time we got to Phoenix (as the old Glen Campbell song goes), we were roasting. It has been touching the upper 90s and low 100s for much of the last couple of weeks in Southern Arizona, so our departure is probably a couple of weeks overdue.

Flagstaff is a quirky place. As we gassed up upon entering town we glimpsed a sign at the Quality Inn next door which read: "No Train Noise/Martians Welcome." Either there is a great big Star Wars convention here or we've entered another dimension. We checked into the England House late this afternoon. Our host welcomed us with a thirty-minute diatribe on what we shouldn't even think of doing here because someone else once did it and it obviously pissed him off. Don't bleed on the throw pillows. Don't park your car unless the right headlight lines up with the planter. Don't bend the big key in the small lock. Don't drink too much alcohol in Flagstaff because the altitude (7,000 feet) magnifies the impact (he was right about that, we realized, as we stumbled home from dinner at the local brewery). Of course he said nothing about the television sets (because there are none, even though the last episode of *House* airs tonight and there is nothing else for us to do in Flagstaff) or the train noise (evidently that's why the Martians don't stay here). Thought we might catch a movie at the local Orpheum theatre. As we strolled up to the marquee the featured presentation was (and I kid you not): "Cattle Decapitation" (see the photo if you don't believe me). Perhaps this is the preferred form of Martian entertainment? A closer inspection indicated that the Orpheum was a theater and Cattle Decapitation is a band. Thank goodness.

More tomorrow when we return from the Gorgeous Gorge.

Hittners Survive Grand Canyon Drive-by

Day 2 (Tuesday, May 22, 2012): Flagstaff, AZ to Grand Canyon and back (170 miles)

First, to calm the collective nerves of our readers, I can reliably report here and now that I was not the Grand Canyon male visitor who plunged 600 feet to his death at the Grand Canyon today. We actually drove by the site of the accident a short time after its occurrence. Dozens of emergency vehicles were a clear indication that something was awry. Later, shortly after our return to Flagstaff, a biker was hit by a car and carted away by ambulance in front of our B&B. What's next, cattle decapitation? *Hmm, we're gonna be extra careful tomorrow!*

As is obvious by this point, the Hittners managed to visit the **Stupendously Enormous Hole** today and returned unscathed. We drove the 85 or so miles from Flagstaff to the eastern entrance of the park and worked our way west by auto, visiting several of the vistas along the way. At the suggestion of our really anal B&B host, we stopped at his "secret" access point (and followed all of his directions, including relevant prohibitions and parking instructions). It involved a one-mile walk up a restricted access road which ended on a ledge with no railings or restraints. No thanks. With winds gusting to 30 or 40 mph today, I was reminded of my days during the summer of 1967 when I served as a college apprentice to an electrician in my father's electrical workers' union. I was assigned to help the old codger string wiring along the perimeter of each floor of a forty-story NYC building then under construction (and therefore completely open at every edge). As he stood on a six-foot ladder on the edge, I cowered wimpily (yes,

that's a word) from a safe distance. Today's experience was a bit of an unwelcome flashback. While Peggy didn't seem uncomfortable, I was less than thrilled at the prospect of blowing over the South Rim. Which one of us is normal?

Later, we made our way to the famous **El Tovar Lodge** for lunch. Advised in advance that they'd stop serving at 2 PM, we hightailed it from our parking space down the road and up several flights of stairs, arriving at the restaurant dripping and gasping for air. Made it by five minutes (though we didn't smell so good). Nice experience, though surprised by the 54-cent surcharge *for utilities* added to the lunch check. After lunch, we sauntered along the rim walkway to several other historic buildings (including the **Kolb Photography Studio**) before calling it a day and driving back to Flagstaff from the opposite direction. For those of you who haven't seen it yet, the enormity of the Grand Canyon is almost unfathomable (as is the penchant for dumbass visitors to perch on stone walls and precipices for what could become their memorial photos). All in all, a good day. Tomorrow, Peggy and Art do Las Vegas!

P.S.- The Tempur-Pedic mattress was pretty nice (though the freight trains kept me up most of the night anyway).

"No, I won't back up!"

Another glimpse into the Humongous Hole

Eggs, Mermaids and The Sin City

Day 3 (Wednesday, May 23, 2012): Flagstaff, AZ to Las Vegas (252 miles)

I awoke suddenly this morning on my Tempur-Pedic mattress is the midst of a very strange dream. I was working late one night at the office when I got hungry. One of my colleagues had just bought a special jumbo-sized egg at the supermarket for $6. It was called a "Yani". I thought an egg would be great so I set off for the market. As is typical in dreams, it took forever to get there but I finally arrived. I walked to the egg desk but no one was there. A nearby employee explained that the counter was closed for the night and she couldn't help me.

Alas, no one could help me. I made some comment about how the world was getting a trifle specialized when only an egg specialist could sell me an egg. I asked to see the manager. I was told he'd be on the floor in 15 minutes and could discuss the matter then. I complained that I'd already invested too much time in this egg thing and how did I know another 15 minutes would yield the results I sought? Finally, the manager appeared. Together we noticed something flopping around on the floor. The manager checked it out. It was, naturally, a mermaid. He helped her up and explained that I needed to take her home and put her in a bathtub. I wasn't too hot on that because I didn't know what to tell my wife and (worst of all) the mermaid was homely. That's when I woke up with a start on said Tempur-Pedic mattress. Why did I relate all of this? Either to ask your collective opinions on what it means or (more likely) to warn you all against buying a Tempur-Pedic mattress.

"Gotta be a way to get in there!"

Another molten chocolate cake

"That painting is alive!"

No intelligent caption possible.

After unburdening myself of the details of my dream, we left our erstwhile bed & breakfast in Flagstaff this morning heading west. We made it to **Kingman, Arizona**, for lunch where (no surprise here) I had eggs. It occurred to us by this time that we were already on our third day of travel and we still hadn't left the intellectually bereft though geologically well-endowed State of Arizona. Determined to finally leave the state of our departure we headed northwest into **Nevada** (a state, as the photo of a Las Vegas cab on the prior page confirms, that is as batty as the one we just left). The corridor around **Lake Mead** (and the **Hoover Dam**) is beautiful, but we saw relatively little of it thanks to the smoky haze which floated southward from a series of forest fires near Reno. For the record, when we finally pulled into the entrance of **The Bellagio Hotel** in **Las Vegas** by mid-afternoon (after *three* days of travel) we were 27 miles *further* from our destination than we were when we started. When the money runs out we're more likely to make it as Walmart greeters than as travel agents.

Leave it to Sin City to trump (no pun intended) the Big Hole. Our early aggravations notwithstanding, Art & Peggy were determined to do it up in Las Vegas. A veteran of one prior visit (none for Peggy), I proceeded to introduce my wife to the **Strip** (again, no pun intended). It was 96 degrees today but we made one quick pass down a portion of the Strip before commencing our own five-hour version of Vegas sensory overload consisting of dinner at **Olives** (a scotch, some Sangria [we drank twice as much to compensate for the lower altitude], grilled vegetable gazpacho, gnocchi in an heirloom tomato ragu with pulled chicken and basil oil and a molten chocolate lava cake dessert), theater (a sparkling presentation of **Jersey Boys** at the **Paris Theatre**—who knew that Frankie Valli and The Four Seasons created so many memorable songs?) and a mind-bending performance of the dancing waters atop the manmade lake outside of our hotel (a music and light-themed spectacle produced by 1,214 shooting fountains and 4,792 lights and no, I didn't count them). All in all it was night well spent and thoroughly enjoyed.

Tomorrow we head to **Zion National Park** in **Utah**. Positively no eggs for breakfast.

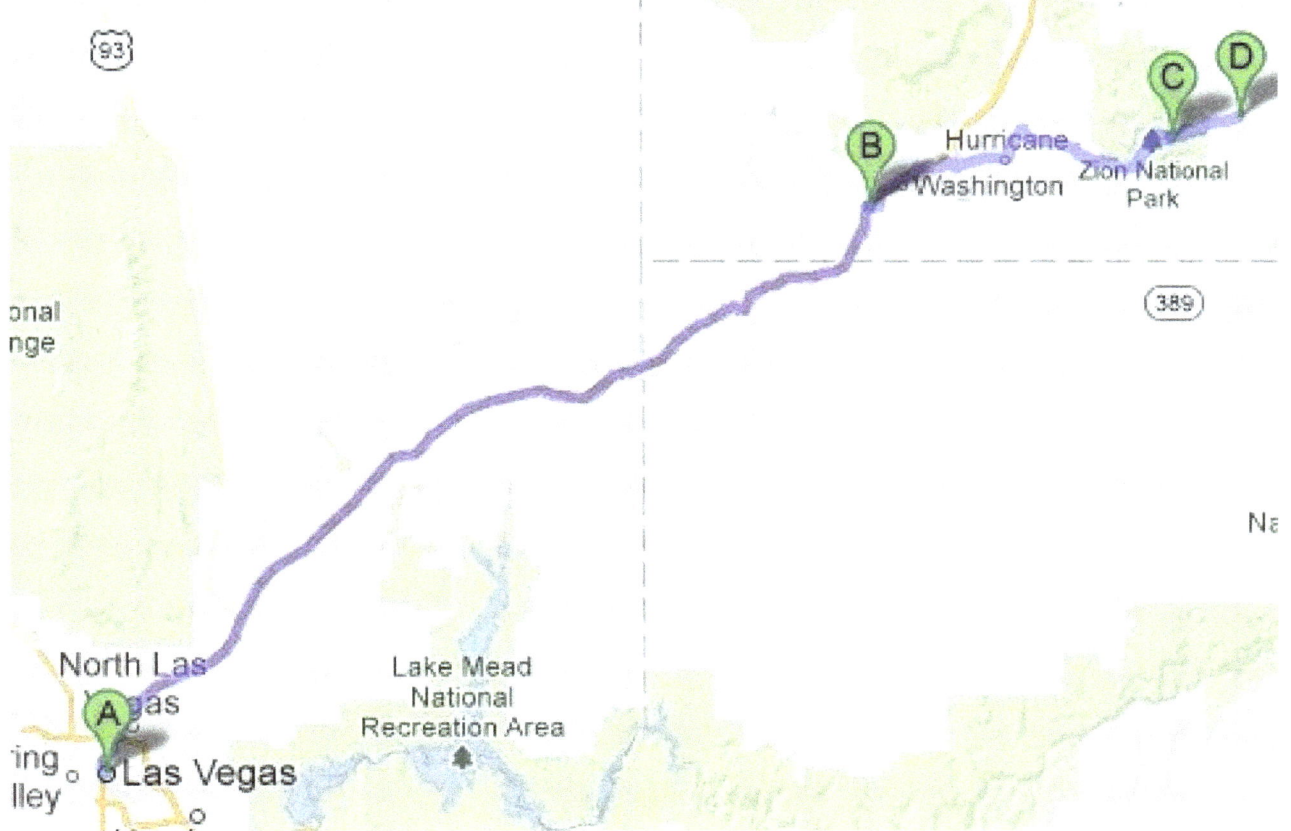

Where Chocolate Flows and Romney Glows

Day 4 (Thursday, May 24, 2012): Las Vegas, NV to St. George, UT, Zion National Park and Mt. Carmel, UT (185 miles)

Tough tearing ourselves away from the wildly excessive yet thoroughly addictive luxury of **The Bellagio**. Breakfast this morning consisted of a delectable vanilla scone from the sinful selection in the **Jean Philippe Patisserie** in the lobby where they torture chocoholics with a multi-chocolate fountain display featuring floor-to-ceiling streams of luscious dark, white and milk chocolate (see photo on page 65). Moments later we experienced an Alice-in-Wonderland moment as we strolled through the courtyard gardens which are arranged and sculpted into stunning floral displays complementing giant Chihuly glass flowers and a merry-go-round. In Vegas, my friends, this is truly the place to stay (assuming you can get the almost laughable internet price we obtained). With our departure, however, reality set in. First, we descended the elevator with a well-dressed guy carrying a ridiculously oversized Versace shopping bag who was obviously unmoved by the Trader Joe's bag in our grasp. Then, retrieving our car from the valet, a large

The Court of the Patriarchs, one of many vistas within Zion National Park in Utah

chunk of plastic molding tumbled unceremoniously from the door frame before we sheepishly escaped the garage.

Back on the road again, we headed north toward **Zion National Park** (another day, another national park). Before arriving, we stopped in the Utah town of **St. George** (hometown of former Red Sox hurler Bruce Hurst). Amazing town. I felt like Jim Carrey's character in The Truman Show: everything there was too good to be real. All new buildings, not a scrap of litter in the perfectly manicured streets. Even the gas stations were spotless. All this against a backdrop of vivid red stone bluffs and hills. But we knew that we were in Romney country and that machine-gun-toting libertarian nutcases were probably lurking behind the phony commercial facades. Fortunately, we left town before anyone could spot our Massachusetts plates.

We did our tour of **Zion** on a beautiful, comfortable, summer-like afternoon. We ambled down a few short trails at various points along the shuttle bus route and enjoyed (and quickly exhausted) ourselves. There was, however, a strange sense of disorientation as we seemed to be about the only couple (other than a few Brits and Aussies) conversing in English. We finished our day by driving across (and even through) the mountains to our lodging at **Zion Mountain Ranch** in **Mt. Carmel, Utah**, on the other (east) side of the park. Now I sit writing in a very pleasant log cabin overlooking the mountains and a broad plain on which a bunch of horses and a small herd of buffalo roam, mate and poop (not necessarily in that order).

Tomorrow, we're taking the yellow brick road on to **Salt Lake City**.

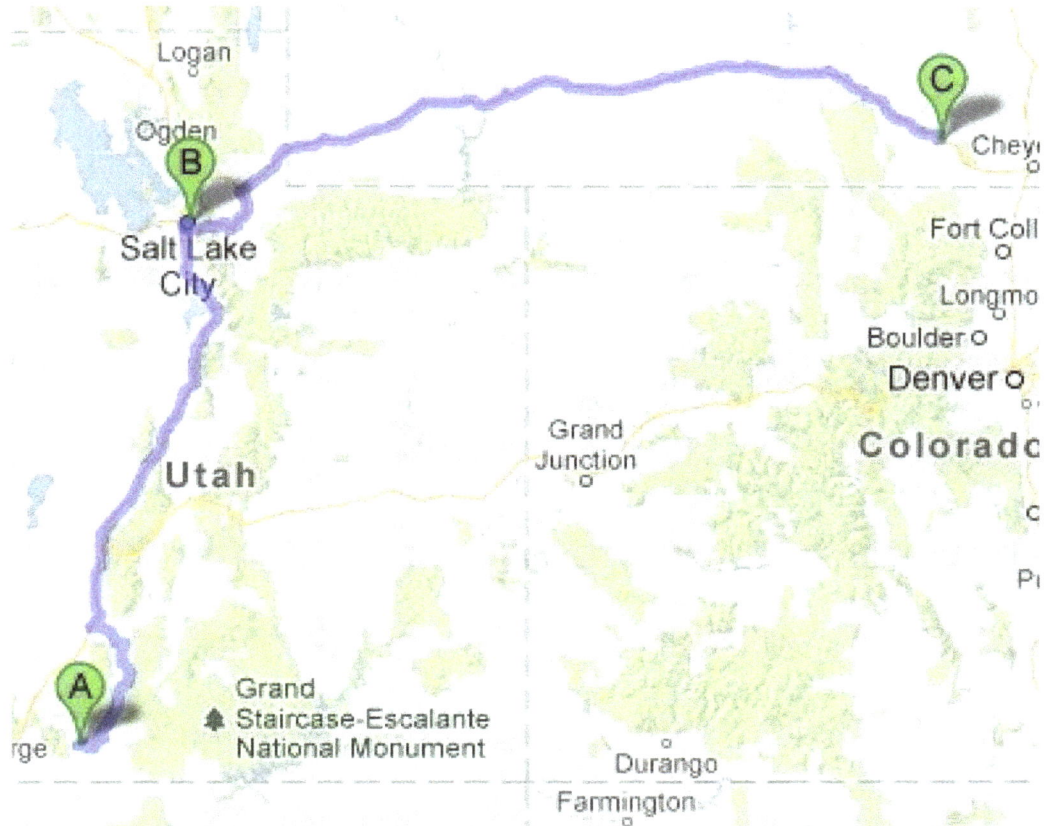

Blowin' Through Wyomin'

Days 5 & 6 (Friday/Saturday, May 25-26, 2012): Mt. Carmel, UT to Salt Lake City, UT (304 miles) and Salt Lake City, UT to Laramie, WY (392 miles)

No, we didn't fall off the face of the earth (or into another big western hole). So here are two days worth of reports from the hinterlands…

We left our cabin amongst the bison droppings near Zion and headed north to visit one of my fraternity brothers (and his wife) in **Salt Lake City**. The drive through the center of **Utah** was often breathtaking. Gorgeous mountains, valleys and not a whole lot of people until you reach **Provo** and (just a little further north) Salt Lake City. Upon arriving, we were treated to a quick tour of the nearby ski areas including a stop at **Park City**. Never wanted to ski there but always curious as to what it looked like. Our hosts decided to take us on the scenic route back home so we navigated a road (the Guardian Pass?) which rose to dizzying and thoroughly unprotected heights (where I had that familiar Grand Canyon feeling

A streetcorner in old downtown Laramie

again). We drove along narrow paved and unnervingly unpaved roads with major league drop-offs. We saw snow banks and majestic stands of aspens, but not a single polygamist (is that an oxymoron?).

After a few too many waffles for breakfast this morning, we bade our gracious hosts goodbye and finally headed east (had to do so eventually) by traversing most of the state of **Wyoming**. We drove almost 400 miles along Route 80 through southern Wyoming (through wind gusts measuring 40-50 mph at times), completing the day's journey in **Laramie**. A bit unsettling as we watched the big trucks wave in the wind at 75 mph while preparing to pass. Fortunately, we made it to Laramie by late afternoon. Upon arrival, we rushed over to the art museum on the campus of the **University of Wyoming** where we took in a nice exhibit of American Regionalist prints, mostly from the 1930s (Thomas Hart Benton and some lesser known but talented artists and including several WPA prints). Worth the stop.

As I write this tonight we are staying at the **Mad Carpenter Inn**, a bed-and-breakfast near the center of Laramie. We've got our own free-standing, pseudo-Victorian cottage here, on two floors. While this place is relatively new and quite nice, the general neighborhood is a bit of a dump (mostly run-down student rentals built in the 1920s and 30s). There is absolutely no evidence of lawn mower ownership. We had dinner at a funky downtown restaurant and walked it off along the downtown streets (a mishmash of nice late 19th century commercial buildings and boxy storefronts from the 1920s). One hopeful sign (and a pleasant counterpoint to the prevalent political culture in this part of the country) was the presence of an Obama campaign office in a downtown storefront. Probably staffed by college students too young to vote. Tomorrow we eschew the interstates and drive back roads some 300 miles north to Mt. Rushmore. We are unarmed so wish us luck.

An inscription on Register Cliff

A tasty purple pie from the Purple Pie Place

Sexy Tractors and Crazy Horses

Day 7 (Sunday, May 27, 2012): Laramie, WY to Rapid City, SD (313 miles)

When driving along the two-lane highways of eastern Wyoming you've got to tune into country music (it's not as if you have a choice). So today's audience participation activity is to vote for your favorite country music song lyric. Here are our nominations gleaned from today's radio offerings (I kid you not):

"Way down yonder in Chatahoochie it gets hotter than a hootchie kootchie"
"She thinks my tractor's sexy"
"Girl, you make my speakers go boom! boom!"

Draw your own conclusions on meaning and send me your votes by reply email.

We spent all but about twenty minutes today on two-lane roads on our journey from **Laramie, Wyoming** to our ultimate destination of **Rapid City, South**

Dakota. There was zero traffic and enthralling (and ever-changing) scenery. Our first stop (on a whim) was **Register Cliff**, a landmark on the National Register of Historic Places located just outside the tiny burg of **Guernsey, Wyoming**. Register Cliff is a soft sandstone cliff along the **Platte River** on the **Oregon Trail** on which emigrants etched their names (and often dates) as they passed through on their western migrations during the mid-nineteenth century. Hundreds, perhaps thousands, of names are chiseled into the stone (along with those of more recent grafitti-addicted copycats). I suspect that the governor of Arizona has sought assurances from Wyoming that the emigrants were legal.

There couldn't have been more than a few hundred actual residents along the highways we covered during the first four hours of our five-hour route. This made finding a lunch stop a bit challenging. The town of **Lusk** (pop. about 1,400) offered the most promise, but each of the three principal restaurants was closed. Fortunately, there was a Subway (the only chain within about a hundred miles, I think) which was open and busy (people gotta eat!). Surprisingly, there were clean bathrooms there, too, although the toilet in the mens' room was so

Crazy Horse sculpture, in progress

Some pretty notable heads at Mt. Rushmore

low (seat height was not more than a foot off the floor!) that I had another of those acrophobic Grand Canyon experiences as I peered in terror all the way down at the (this time small) hole.

As we pulled out of Lusk, one couldn't help to be amazed at the extraordinary cloud formations which filled the expansive blue sky. The photo on page 72 barely begins to convey the impact.

Our dual objectives today were to visit **Mt. Rushmore** and the **Crazy Horse Memorial** (about 20 miles south of Mt. Rushmore) in southwestern South Dakota, but before reaching that target, we stopped at the **Purple Pie Place** in the honky-tonky town of **Custer**. Good choice: nothing refreshes like a great blueberry pie. Place was jumping; they tell me their customers consume 75-150 pies a day. No wonder we have an obesity problem.

On to Crazy Horse. The **Crazy Horse Memorial** is a privately-funded work-in-progress designed by the now deceased (and probably crazy) sculptor Korczak Ziolkowski whose crazy widow and most of their ten crazy children are continuing their effort to construct the largest outdoor sculpture in the world. The sculpture, when and if ever completed, will portray Lakota chief Crazy Horse on his crazy horse. So far, only the warrior's face is complete, though it is impressive (and humongous). The crazy family has constructed a maze of subsidiary museums and outbuildings at the site which contain thousands of Native American artifacts and various displays relating to Native American culture and the ongoing effort to complete the sculpture before the end of time. After an introductory documentary and a quick tour of the museum, we decided to shell out an additional $8 for a bus ride to the base of the sculpture. BIG mistake. We had expected a ten-minute round-trip which would have merely allowed us to take photos from a closer vantage point. Instead we were virtually kidnapped by a bus driver who was crazier than Crazy Horse or his crazy horse. After we were herded into an old yellow schoolbus he introduced himself as a 68-year-old "senior seasonal migrant worker" (huh?) and began babbling about the sculpture and various related topics (all of which were covered in the introductory film or were of no intrinsic interest) for twenty minutes before actually starting the bus. He then steered the bus at glacier speed about a quarter mile up the road pointing out rock piles, "varmints" and launching into his failed nightclub act. About thirty minutes later, he finally let us out of the bus to take pictures. When we returned to our seats we sat in stunned silence as he picked up a wooden flute and obliged us to listen to a white-man's crappy rendition of a sacred Native American tune. When he mercifully returned to the driver's seat he took us on a ten-minute tour of the parking lot before finally releasing us forty-five minutes after the tour began (by this time he had begun to repeat himself by retelling the same stories and crummy jokes). The only thing worse than a crazy bus driver is a crazy senior bus driver with dementia. When the torture ended so did our visit.

Having spent entirely too long with the Crazies, we rushed back to the car and headed up the road to **Mt. Rushmore**, hoping to get a glimpse of the presidential quartet before dark. After Crazy Horse, the much smaller, less ambitious Mt. Rushmore was underwhelming at best. To me, Teddy Roosevelt looked like a kindly old retiree interloper who happened into the picture when Washington, Jefferson and Lincoln were being portrayed for posterity.

Following our brief Mt. Rushmore experience, we drove another twenty miles to **Rapid City** where we had booked a room in a downtown historic hotel. We had dinner in an old firehouse and were impressed with the charm and level of activity in downtown Rapid City on a Sunday evening. As for the hotel, it is not on our recommended list (especially for the tall and/or hefty). The room is the size of our bathroom at the Bellagio. The miniscule bathroom came equipped with a used washcloth hanging over the top of the shower stall, a missing towel rack and a two-flush toilet (i.e., took two flushes to...well, you get it). On the plus side, it is efficient: you can sit on the toilet and wash up at the same time while opening a 1923 bottle of Coke (if you happen to have one) with the long-outdated bottle opener on the wall. The sink was nearly at my knee level (good luck to six-footers) and there was no clearance below the toiletry shelf to operate the faucet. The wi-fi was free but non-operational (which will explain why this email won't go out until tomorrow morning).

Tomorrow threatens to be our most boring day, with nothing more than a 350-mile journey from Rapid City to Sioux Falls on the agenda (though we might make a quick stop at the famous **Wall Drug** in **Wall, SD**). You'll need to wait until tomorrow night to find out just how boring it turns out to be. Until then, don't forget to vote for your favorite country music lyric nominated above!

Wall Drug Wonders and the Flying Trashcan

Day 8 (Monday, May 28, 2012): Rapid City, SD to Sioux Falls, SD (350 miles)

First of all, in the absence of a groundswell of support for any one of my country lyrics, I have elected to award the crown to a lyric nominated by one of our erstwhile readers in Dallas, Texas. The winning ditty goes as follows:

"How can I kiss the lips at night that chewed my ass out all day long?"

The entrance to the enormous Wall Drug superstore in Wall, SD

Now we turn to an account of how the Hittners managed to amuse themselves while driving 350 otherwise nondescript and virtually uninhabited miles across the great state of South Dakota.

Within minutes of accessing Interstate 90, the signs began to appear. "Free Ice Water at Wall Drug"; "5 Cent Coffee at Wall Drug" and the like. A grand total of 61 signs (who's already bored?) in the 50 or so miles from Rapid City to **Wall, South Dakota**. We had been urged by some of our readers to make a stop at the famous **Wall Drug** complex so stop we did. For the Wall Drug virgins among you, it is (according to Wikipedia and the *New York Times*, respectively) "a cowboy-themed shopping mall/department store" that has become "a sprawling tourist attraction of international renown [which generates] more than $10 million a year and draws some two million annual visitors to [the] remote town" of Wall, SD (population 821) located along Interstate 90 east of Rapid City. Wall Drug easily amused us with its folksy kitsch and random inventory for almost an hour. It has everything imaginable, from a collection of Western art (ranging from the sublime, including original N.C. Wyeths and Dean Cornwells, to painted velvet-quality cowboy art) to its own version of Bellagio's dancing waters (lame by comparison, of course). We got off easy: two tee shirts and a belt (made in China).

The famous Flying Trashcan (see text, next page)

The wild and crazy lady at the Corn Palace

A couple of hours after returning to the interstate we began searching for a lunch stop. We limited our search to towns with more than 500 residents. So we stopped at the **Star Family Restaurant** (AAA rated!) in **Murdo** (pop. 533). This place was built, and remains firmly grounded, in the Fifties. We passed on the biscuits and gravy special and gravitated for the safety of pancakes and eggs. While awaiting our meals, a kid in the next booth blew lunch, which just added to the charm of

The Corn Palace, Mitchell, South Dakota

the place. After lunch, I stopped in the mens' room where I witnessed a rather unusual phenomenon. A particularly loud and powerful hot air hand-drying machine was positioned directly above a trash can with a centrally pivoting flip-top. When I turned on the dryer to dry my hands the trash can top began rotating at Mach 2 speeds and nearly attained lift off. It obviously takes little to amuse me...

Our next target was the first McDonald's in the 200 or so miles since Rapid City. We go there for the jumbo $1 iced teas. Of course the corollary of large ice teas is the need to pee 100 miles later. That took us to **Mitchell, SD**, which is the ancestral home of one of our readers. We chose to pee at Mitchell's famous **Corn Palace** (see photo above) which has its roots (no pun intended) in a corn-centric exposition which began in 1892 (organized by our reader's great grandparents). Today's Corn Palace is a castle-like multi-purpose facility which hosts basketball games, displays corn-related exhibitions and sells corny kitsch. Perhaps most notable are the numerous outdoor and inside murals made of cornhusks and corn cobs. Surprisingly good, but not likely to join the Hittner collection anytime soon.

Leaving Fort Fructose we headed to Sioux Falls where we're spending the night at a rather conventional, newly-opened Holiday Inn Express.

We're now about half way home. Tomorrow is Tuesday so it must be Minneapolis. We'll likely resume our travelogue in a couple of days when we reach Milwaukee.

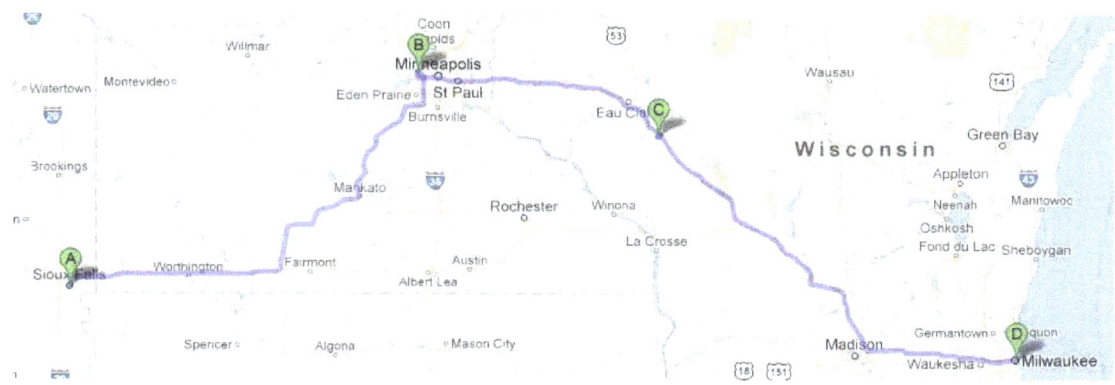

Roadkill and Other Norwegian Treats

Days 9 & 10 (Tuesday/Wednesday, May 29-30, 2012): Sioux Falls, SD to Plymouth, MN (243 miles) and Plymouth, MN to Milwaukee, WI (353 miles)

One of the unwritten rules of the road (at least for the Hittners) is to go easy in print on those who have graciously hosted us, lest we wind up in even more Holiday Inns (or worse). "Can't wait to read what you say about us!!" wrote one of our friends (nervously) just this morning. Our wonderful hosts and hostesses can rest easy, as we've had a great time visiting friends in Salt Lake City, Minneapolis and (tonight) Milwaukee. We won't write about [deleted] or [deleted], so don't worry! We had a great time last night with Peggy's childhood friends and a pair of newer friends from Tucson who summer in Minneapolis. Tonight we joined another couple from Tucson for drinks at their Milwaukee loft followed by an excellent dinner several miles north on the Milwaukee lakefront (which is beautiful).

Since our last epistle we've driven from **Sioux Falls** to **Minneapolis**, much of it along two- and four-lane rural highways through picture-perfect farm country, and today from **Minneapolis** to **Milwaukee** along one interminably long interstate. Today was probably the most boring ride to date on our equally interminable journey. How boring was it? So boring that we kept track of roadkill: seven deer and almost thirty unidentified furry creatures divided almost evenly between the left and right sides of the road. During one particularly grisly patch of interstate just west of **Madison** at least a dozen unidentified furries bit the proverbial dust. We also counted mobile barns (see photo on the title page of this volume) but maxed out at only one.

At the suggestion of our Minneapolis hosts, we stopped today for lunch at the famous **Norske Nook Bakery & Restaurant** in bustling **Osseo, Wisconsin**. Dripping with Norwegianism (the quality of being very Norwegian), the NNB&R was everything you'd imagine it to be: quaint, a little cheesy (no pun intended), staffed with over-ripe girl-next-door blondes from Osseo serving big cholesterol-laden hunks of pie (they claim to have won 23 national pie awards) to a room full of old folks and ankle-biters. For you techies they even offered some Norwegian humor (another apparent oxymoron): e.g., the definitions of "log on" ("makin' da vood stove hotter!"); or "modem" ("vat yew did tew da hay fields"). Not surprisingly, the restaurant is situated just down the block from several quilting establishments and an antique shop with a "gone fishing" sign on the front door. In front of the local church was a large sign assuring Nels that the entire congregation stood behind him. It doesn't get much more authentic than this...

Tomorrow morning we hit two Milwaukee museums before hitting the road again, this time heading to **South Bend, Indiana**. More reports tomorrow...

The Norske Nook: Dripping with Norwegianism

Art Imitates Life

We thought some of you might be intrigued to see a pair of photos which clearly demonstrate the connection between art and life. Appearing below left is a photo taken at the Norske Nook (the restaurant which was described in the preceding entry). On the following day, we saw the painting below right by Wayne Thiebaud at the Milwaukee Museum of Art. The relationship is amusing.

Norse Nook, daily pie display, mixed media (assorted fruit, crust, whipped cream, etc.), 2012

Wayne Thiebaud, "Refrigerator Pies," oil on canvas, 1962 (Milwaukee Museum of Art)

Milwaukee in Drag

Day 11 (Thursday, May 31, 2012): Milwaukee, WI to South Bend, IN (186 miles)

Our good weather fortune couldn't last forever. Nor could our record of clear sailing on the highways. We got the double whammy today.

We spent the morning hitting two Milwaukee museums, the **Milwaukee Museum of Art** (fabulous building, decent but not overwhelming collection) and the sleeper of this trip, the **Grohmann Museum**. The Grohmann is situated on the campus of the **Milwaukee School of Engineering** and consists of over 800 paintings and sculptures by principally European and (some) American artists which celebrate various aspects of men (and women) at work. The works were collected by Eckhardt Grohmann, a German-born engineer and Milwaukee entrepreneur who

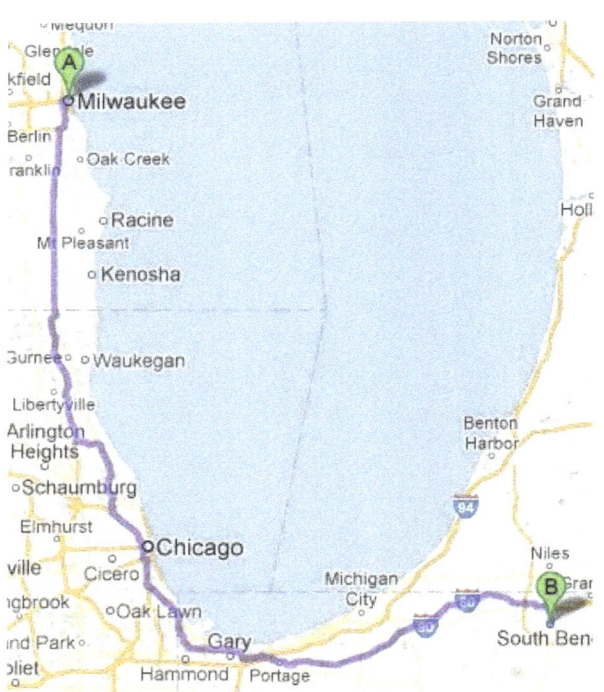

donated his collection to the school. The quality of the works is outstanding; they range in date from the 1500s to about 2007. The collection is housed in a modern, four-story building in downtown Milwaukee. Just for the record, however, downtown Milwaukee is a total drag, shabby and unattractive---all of which terms aptly describe certain of the women (or not?) that we encountered around the hotel.

As soon as we hit the highway south the rain began, along with ubiquitous road construction and ever-increasing traffic. We spent at least an hour and a half (involuntarily) trying to make it through the city of Chicago en route to **South Bend, Indiana**, our destination for this evening (and where we plan to see an art museum on the Notre Dame campus in the morning). The rain still continues as I write this and it promises to keep us company as we drive to Cleveland tomorrow. On the plus side, South Bend (so far) is quite nice. We'll see about Cleveland...

One of the heroic bronze figures depicting men at work which comprise the rooftop sculpture garden display at the Grohmann Museum in Milwaukee.

Not Quite Shaker Heights

Day 12 (Friday, June 1, 2012): South Bend, IN to Cleveland, OH (256 miles)

We enjoyed a comfortable night and a hearty breakfast at our bed & breakfast in **South Bend, Indiana**. At breakfast we met a very nice older guest who was attending his 58th Notre Dame reunion. He told us that people of his vintage are invited to reunion every year as what he termed "prospective decedents," i.e., alumni whose impending demise stands a good chance of enriching the college's coffers.

Our hosts were a couple in their late 40s, the wife more amiable than the husband. She seemed to be constantly supplementing his list of outdoor chores while correcting him on each piece of information he gave us in response to our questions about Notre Dame. I suspect one of them bludgeoned the other to death after our departure.

After checking out, we drove the three or four miles to the **University of Notre Dame** campus, passed the hallowed football stadium and visited the **Snite Museum of Art**. What a wonderful college art museum! Though modest in size, the museum had outstanding examples of art from all periods and cultures including (of particular interest to us) some wonderful Taos School works by Victor Higgins and Walter Ufer, some fine Native American artifacts and a pair of large wooden carved tablets by American modernist William Zorach. Overall, it was an hour very well spent.

Returning to the road, we headed east toward **Cleveland** in a dreary, persistent mist, stopping only for gas and then for lunch at an Olive Garden near Toledo. We elected to split a chicken panini ($8.95) and received with it (at no extra charge, of course) a big bowl of minestrone, a bowl of salad the size of a basketball and enough bread to choke a horse. I'm convinced that these restaurants have conspired to keep America obese: in addition to serving humongous meals they accommodate humongous customers by putting wheels on their chairs to make it easier for them to get up after dinner.

When we'd finished lunch, we completed our drive to Cleveland (much easier than yesterday's interminable journey through Chicago). We had tried last night without success to reserve a room at one of several bed and breakfasts in Cleveland. One of the proprietors told us that although he was full, he had another "extended stay" property just a mile or so away and close to the Cleveland Museum of Art (which we had planned on visiting). He said nothing about its

The "deftly engineering heating and cooling system" at our sketchy Cleveland lodging

location in what I would delicately term a "developing neighborhood". When we exited the highway and headed into the city toward the designated address we became increasingly squeamish. Talk about sketchy. We're staying in a house from the Twenties or so with several other unidentified guests reportedly occupying other rooms in the house (one is a German couple visiting a son at **Case Western University**; they probably think this is payback for WWII). The place is furnished in the furniture our parents discarded a generation ago. For a glimpse of the deftly engineered heating and cooling system, see the photo on the preceding page.

Upon our arrival, we were met by a woman who promptly instructed us in the methodology for working our way through the sequence of locks required to permit entry into this fortress. Then, in response to my halting inquiry about neighborhood security, she assured us that it had to be safe because they paid someone to cruise the area 24 hours a day. If that doesn't put you at ease, what will? This isn't Shaker Heights!

After our orientation, we drove the couple of miles to the **Cleveland Art Museum** where we were among a very select group of attendees (the guards dramatically outnumbered the visitors). The museum is undergoing substantial construction and renovation which may partially explain the lack of attendance. Curiously, almost nothing created after 1925 is on display (a big disappointment to us, of course). However, the American and European collections (particularly the French Impressionists, Picasso, Gauguin, etc.) were outstanding and well worth the visit.

At the suggestion of the woman who had admitted us into our sketchy lodging, we had dinner at **Felice's**, a trendy restaurant three doors down which is apparently a hot urban find which attracts upwardly mobile urban pioneers to this developing frontier. It is probably fair to assume that the residents of this neighborhood were not particularly well represented among their clientele. It was ridiculously busy (though it is a Friday night), reasonably good and served our favorite dessert, chocolate lava cake (this was the third time our vulnerability to this delicacy has been exploited during this trip).

Fortunately, the car was still parked outside the fortress upon our return this evening. Hopefully, it will be there tomorrow, tires, doors and all.

Big Al, Rock & Roll and the Institution

Day 13 (Saturday, June 2, 2012): Cleveland, OH to Chautauqua, NY (135 miles)

We awoke yesterday (Saturday) to unexpected sunshine and the continued (if not surprising) presence of our undisturbed vehicle. Perhaps no respectable criminal would be interested in a car fastened together with duct tape.

After showering and dressing we headed downstairs to find our German housemates huddled around the dining table with their son, a doctoral candidate in mathematics at Case Western. They seemed nice enough but perhaps we're blind to the realities here. They say they're headed out to downtown Cleveland; perhaps they are terrorists plotting to blow up the Rock & Roll Hall of Fame! And as for our landlord, I don't think he ever had a bed and breakfast that was full; I think he just lures unsuspecting tourists to this house to recruit them for terrorist acts. Thank goodness we're leaving...

But before we leave there's the matter of breakfast. We venture out a couple of doors down to **Big Al's** at Larchmere and 126th. This is the absolute definition of a hole-in-the-wall diner. Unlike Felice's (last night's dinner destination), this place is frequented by the locals and has the feel of a neighborhood institution. And the food is good (see the photo on page 89 of Peggy enjoying her morning joe at Big Al's). Now that we're about to leave, I'm beginning to become more enamored of the neighborhood. And maybe the Germans aren't terrorists after all (they *were* pretty nice people). But I'm still not sure about the landlord...

You can't leave Cleveland without checking out the **Rock & Roll Hall of Fame** (see photo below). We drove into the city (different world here) and visited this venerable lakeside attraction. In this sparkling piece of architecture with six floors of exhibits we spent an entertaining hour and a half working our way through our musical memories.

The drive from Cleveland to **Chautauqua, New York** takes us through three states (Ohio, Pennsylvania and New York) in a couple of hours. We are visiting friends of Peggy's who spend the summers at her friend's mother's house in **Chautauqua Institution**, a strange name for a spectacular summer community and arts destination located on a beautiful lake in the southwestern corner of New York State near Jamestown. Established as a religious community in 1874, this idyllic hamlet is the host of a nine-week program of lectures, concerts and related activites each summer. We got a tour of the grounds from our hosts, had a

scrumptious chicken lasagna dinner and then attended a free band and choral concert in the Institution's wonderful outdoor amphitheater. This place is truly special; we need to come back here sometime when the summer program is in session.

The rain is back so it looks like it will be a dreary ride to Corning (or perhaps Ithaca), New York today (Sunday). We should be home on Monday and you will no longer be burdened by my cross-country ruminations. Yeah!

Big Al's Diner (left) isn't much from the outside but is a warm and friendly neighborhood fixture within

Bronco Busting

Day 14 (Sunday, June 3, 2012): Chautauqua, NY to Ithaca, NY (204 miles)

We're sitting here at the **William Henry Miller Inn**, a very pleasant bed and breakfast in **Ithaca, New York**. After an outstanding brunch with our **Chautauqua** friends, we headed off to Ithaca by way of **Corning, New York** through a whole lot of raindrops. The rain let up briefly (and conveniently) as we pulled into Corning where we visited the **Rockwell Museum of Western Art**. Our fifth art museum in five days, the Rockwell did not disappoint. It is a Western art-only venue with a very good collection of historic and contemporary works including excellent examples by Sharp, Leigh, Wyeth, Blumenschein, Russell and Remington as well as living Native American artists. Amazingly, we saw our *fourth* example of Remington's famous *Bronco Buster* sculpture out of the five art museums we visited on this trip. One day, perhaps, the Tucson Museum of Art will have a collection comparable to the Rockwell, though that may take some doing.

In Ithaca we lucked out: the rain stopped, allowing us to stroll through the downtown streets which were closed to accommodate an annual street fair. We also had a great tapas dinner at **Just a Taste**, a small downtown restaurant recommended by our innkeeper. Back here at the inn we couldn't resist the complimentary desserts. With all our driving, eating and lack of exercise for the past two weeks we'll both have some 'splaining to do when we hit the

Downtown Ithaca, New York was hosting its annual street fair

scales. Hopefully the weigh stations along the highway will be closed until we complete our odyssey.

Tomorrow morning we embark upon the final leg of this, our longest cross-country trip (out of the six we've taken during the last three years). Our mileage figure for this trip will approach 4,000 (the most direct possible route would have been only about 2,700 miles). I suppose when you drive west instead of east you can put on as many extra miles as we have pounds (well, hopefully not that many). But it has been fun and we've seen many new places and enjoyed (mostly) our share of new adventures.

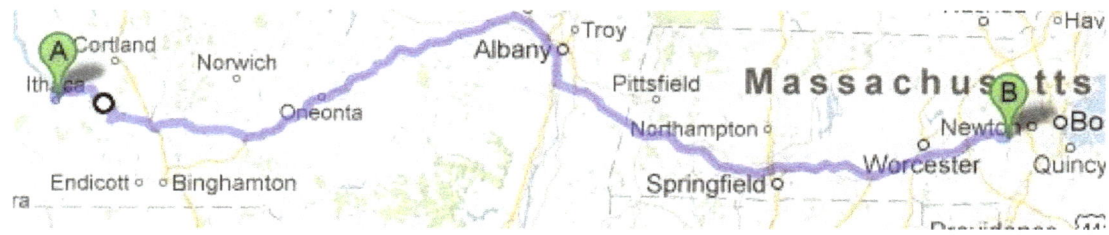

Home Again!

Day 15 (Monday, June 4, 2012): Ithaca, NY to Natick, MA (325 miles)

Just to close the loop for all of our readers waiting breathlessly for evidence of our safe arrival, we are here in **Natick, Massachusetts** once again. We arrived home yesterday mid-afternoon after another dismal day of rain-drenched driving. Absolutely nothing worthwhile to report regarding yesterday's uneventful trip. In all, we logged about 3,950 miles on this cross-country caper, a Hittner record, and approximately 46% more mileage than would have been required to get from Tucson to Natick by any logical, direct route. But we definitely had more fun (although 15 days together in a car is probably one or two more than ideal for maintaining a stable marriage).

We are already weary from five consecutive days of constant rain (made worse by the fact that several of the days we already spent in dreariness have caught up with us for a replay). Temperatures here are half of what they were in Tucson (highs in the low 50s). Also, probably as a consequence of age, we've clearly forgotten where everything is here in our Natick condominium so we've spent much of our time here so far figuring out where things were (and where the things we brought back should go). Not to mention the time spent getting the phone, television and internet to work properly. Oh, well, it is only the first day; by the time we get it right it will be time to return to Arizona.

Thanks to all for your patience and tolerance for our daily travel rants and your email comments. See you all sooner or later (depending on your location).

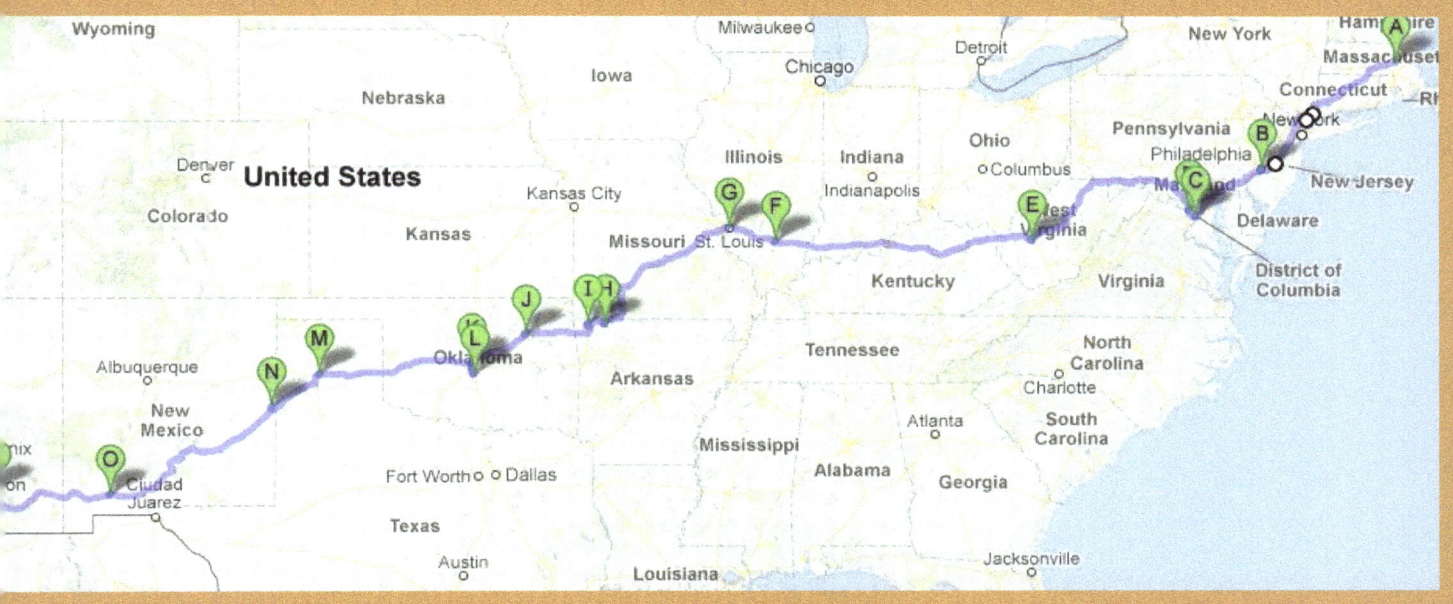

Trip Four

Copulating Cabs and Little Green Men

**Natick, Massachusetts to
Oro Valley (Tucson), Arizona
11 Days, 2,890 Miles
September 28-October 8, 2012**

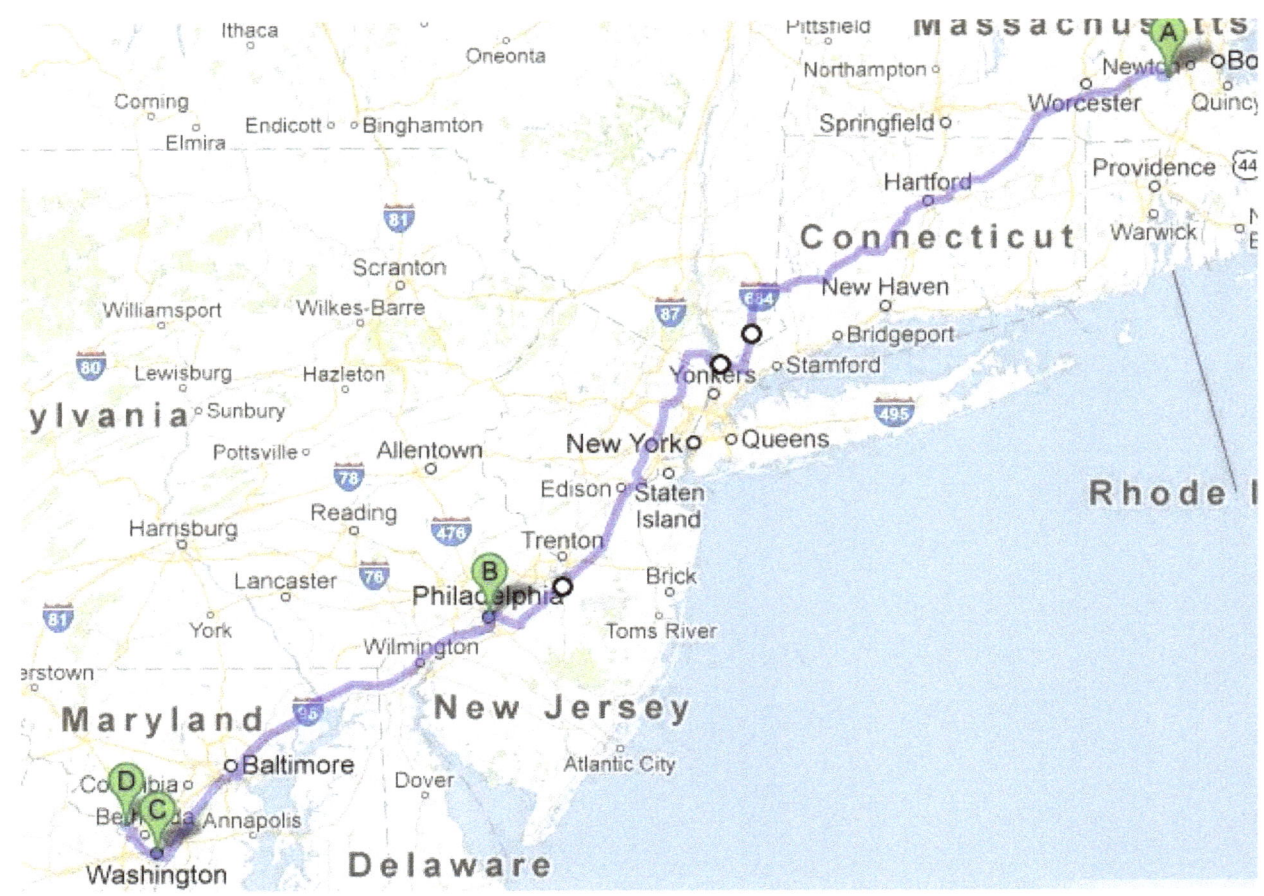

Drought Busting and Fat Lady Lusting

Days 1 & 2 (Friday/Saturday, September 28-29, 2012): Natick, MA to Philadelphia, PA (316 miles) and Philadelphia, PA to Potomac, MD via Washington, DC (159 miles)

It's that time again: time for Peggy and Art to wind their way back to Tucson on deftly selected interstates and a smattering of occasionally colorful two-lane country highways. This year's trip will take us initially down the eastern seaboard, and then across the nation's heartland. We are armed with our trusty roll of duct tape even though our ride has changed from a well-taped 2002 Lexus with 120K miles to a slightly younger (2005) version of the same car with but 42K miles on the odometer. With any luck, we won't need the tape. In any event, you are receiving this because you lack the good sense to request removal from our cross-country chronicles distribution list. So here are the first two days' worth of dispatches from the road to Tucson:

Friday, September 28th: Boston to Philadelphia

I am thoroughly exhausted as I record Day #1 of what started rather ominously as the Art & Peggy Hittner Drought-Busting Cross-Country Tour.

The day began with an early morning detour to the office of Peggy's eye doctor. As a newly-minted geriatric who will join the shiftless 47% sponging off Medicare in October, Peggy was determined to visit her eye doctor before the eye care benefits of her existing medical policy were replaced by the less generous coverages of her new Medicare supplement policy (which kicks in in a couple of days). It was the doctor, however, who proved shiftless, leaving us sitting on our hands for almost two hours while he took an excruciatingly leisurely approach to patient care (or lack thereof). Though the old lady can still see, the endless waiting delayed our departure until nearly lunchtime. By the time we got on the road for our first day's drive to Philadelphia, the day was fit only for amphibians. Like the endless rain which accompanied us during the last five days of our spring trip east, the heavens seemed destined to erase the drought as we prepared to paddle our way back to Tucson.

But alas, the drought will live another day. The rains abated as we passed into New York and New Jersey, only to be replaced by what those states do best: jam up the roads. Stop and go. Ugh! The rains were less aggravating.

We arrived in **Philadelphia** around 6 PM. We squeezed into a miniature parking spot about three blocks from our bed-and-breakfast in the Fairmount Park section of Philadelphia, within walking distance of the Philadelphia Museum of Art and the new **Barnes Foundation Museum**. Our B&B hostess is (inconveniently) out on the town, so she left a key in the flowerpot and we let ourselves in. This particular one-guest-room accommodation is quite attractive, nestled on the upper floor of a renovated townhouse with an adjacent roof deck and our favorite kind of art (American paintings from the Thirties) on the walls. Our kind of place. The owner's name is Mrs. Dych, so I'm still debating how to address her when we meet for breakfast (assuming she'll return home by then). The most obvious pronunciations could be equally embarrassing if incorrect. Guess we'll just say "hi, there".

After self-checking ourselves into our unhosted B&B, we set off to have a bite of dinner (shared some sushi at the local Whole Foods) and to visit the new **Barnes Foundation Museum**. You may have heard of this: the late and eternally cranky inventor and entrepreneur **Dr. Albert Barnes** assembled one of the world's most extensive collections of Impressionist and Post-Impressionist art and hung it in his own cranky way in a Main Line mansion in the town of Merion, just outside of Philadelphia. He despised the Philadelphia elite and resisted all entreaties to move his precious collection to the big city. Before the crank croaked, he established a foundation to assure his collection would remain where it was forever: no one could move it, rehang it or even loan it. Long story short: his foundation went belly-up and he rolled belly-down in his grave as the hated Philadelphia elite hijacked the collection to the big city. As a concession to the croaked crank, the new building housing his collection displays it in room settings absolutely identical (to the inch) to those in which he displayed it in his Main Line mansion.

The visit was interesting. We had been to the old site while Lauren was at Penn. The new installation is the old installation encased in a bigger (modern) building and with many more people paying lots of money ($18 a pop) for the privilege of seeing the collection. Had the old crank not croaked, this would have killed him. It is, however, now accessible to the multitudes, which he would have abhorred, I think. The collection itself is rather incredible. There are more Renoirs and Cezannes than there are firearms in Arizona. Modiglianis, Matisses and Picassos are also abundant and in endless variation. To see it all is to overdose; after a while the fat Renoir female bathers with big butts, enormous busts and pinheads get on your nerves. I suppose old Albert found them attractive--it was his equivalent of internet porn. There are the masterpieces and then there are the garbage-time works by the same masters. By the time we had perambulated our way through the maze of rooms we were pooped. Oh, well, one day, one museum.

It is off to **Washington, D.C.** tomorrow morning!

Saturday, September 29th: Philadelphia to Washington

We enjoyed our Philadelphia accommodation. But our meeting with Mrs. D was like a guided visit from a ghost in *The Christmas Carol.* We learned that all of the 1930's art on the walls (which we much admired) was collected by our hostess' late husband, largely over her objections. So she knew little about it (which she'd come to regret) though she retained it for sentimental reasons. She said she used to get mad at her husband for buying art at the expense of their kid's college fund. So eerily familiar! So this is one view of the future: Art croaked and Peggy retaining Art on the walls (pun intended), running a one-guest B&B and nurturing two old cats and a bird. Please God, let it not come to that!

After a desultory breakfast we hoisted our belongings downstairs and walked the three blocks to our parked car. Fortunately, it was where and how we left it. So we reloaded and headed south to **Washington**. There, we visited Peggy's mom, enjoyed some lunch and headed out for museum #2, the **National Gallery of Art** where we could see a major retrospective of the work of the famous Ashcan School artist **George Bellows**. The exhibit was terrific: Bellows was a master whether painting gritty New York City scenes, grisly boxing matches or seascapes of the Monhegan Island area in Maine. Well worth the visit (the exhibition ends shortly in D.C. and moves to the Metropolitan Museum in New York for any who might be interested).

We covered a lot of real estate getting to the museum and returning, ultimately, to our car. In other words, two days, two museums and two pooped old farts. We dragged ourselves back to the vehicle to join one of Peggy's childhood friends for dinner and a pleasant night's lodging in suburban **Potomac, Maryland**. Tomorrow, we hit the pavement heading west (more or less) through West Virginia. Further reports to follow.

Incidentally, your comments to this (and any subsequent email you receive from us) are welcome. And like all spammers with integrity, we invite you to remove your name from our list by clicking "unsubscribe" below (hah!). And if that works, Romney will win the Hispanic vote!

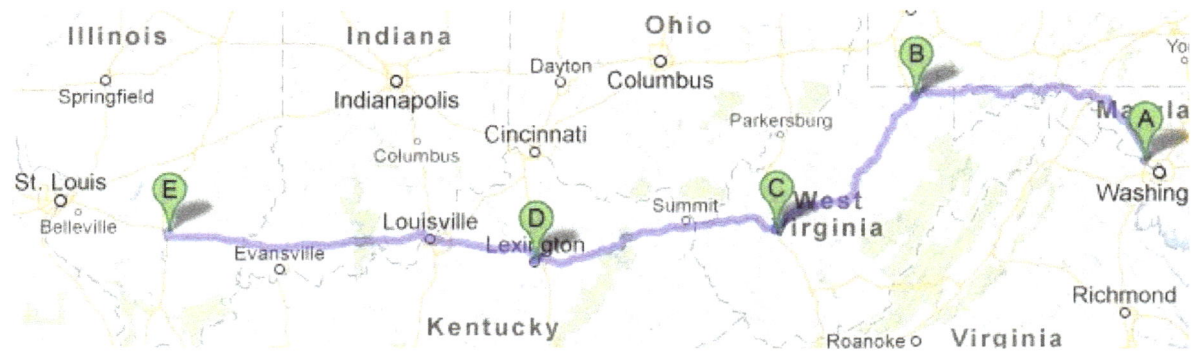

Midwestern Daze : Politically Incorrect in Appalachia

Days 3 & 4 (Sunday/Monday, September 30-October 1, 2012): Potomac, MD to Charleston, WV (349 miles) and Charleston, WV to Mt. Vernon, IL (430 miles)

For those of you with nothing better to do, you can marvel at how I can write so much about so little:

Sunday, September 30th (Washington, D.C. to Charleston, WV):

We're sitting here in a Holiday Inn Express hotel room having just pigged out at a *pair* of mediocre restaurants here in the outskirts of **Charleston, West Virginia**. It was an otherwise uneventful (and museum-less) day spent driving through northern **Maryland** and **West Virginia**. The roads were pleasingly uncrowded for our Sunday jaunt through the beautiful rolling terrain of the **Appalachians**.

Our initial break was a McDonald's pit stop in the town of **Cumberland,** a rather run-down city in northwestern Maryland (14th poorest of 318 metropolitan areas in the U.S.). While awaiting my turn to buy an iced tea, I overheard a crusty old redneck ordering coffee from an innocent-looking teenage girl behind the counter. The repartee went something like this:

Crusty Redneck: "I like it black and hot, just like my women."

Young (White female) Counter Clerk, matter-of-factly: "I hear that all of the time."

Really? The response was hard to explain but the conversation apparently passes for political correctness in this part of America.

Morgantown, West Virginia was our lunch stop. Venturing in to check out the downtown, we found minimal activity on the largely shuttered streets. Lunch, however, was a delightful local delicacy: catfish tacos at the **Golden Finch** on High Street.

Finally, we called it a day in **Charleston**, choosing a predicable hotel in the midst of an endless stream of suburban-style shopping malls. At least two dozen mid-level chain restaurants competed for our dinner dollar. We went with a fairly routine Mexican restaurant, primarily for the promise of ice cold Dos Equis drafts (a promise nicely fulfilled). The boring desserts failed to move us so we hopped over to another chain, **Quaker Steak and Lube**, for a thoroughly unnecessary but substantially more satisfying brownie a la mode. This chain was new to us: it has an automotive motif (gas pump handles serve as door handles while Corvettes (engines removed) are perched on walls and ceilings). Our waitress was (unintentionally) in character: a motor-mouth on high test. We'll undoubtedly regret the combination of Mexican food and brownies in another hour or two. (Another piece of local color: returning to our car outside the restaurant we had to wait for the passenger in the adjoining pickup truck to finish stuffing his lip with a fistful of snuff before he'd shut his door to allow us to enter our car. We waited patiently, knowing, of course, that the pickup was likely well-armed.)

Tomorrow we'll aim for Louisville, Kentucky.

Monday, October 1st (Charleston, WV to Mt. Vernon, IL, wherever that is...)

Peggy and Art have now singlehandedly eliminated the drought in the Midwest. Our Drought-Killing Cross-Country Tour had a banner day, treading bucket loads of water as we floated 430 or so nautical miles through West Virginia, northern Kentucky, southern Indiana and a portion of southern Illinois. We had intended to spend the night in **Louisville, Kentucky**, but floated right on by (didn't make much sense to explore the city in the rain, so we just kept on going). We did, however, make a lunch stop in **Lexington, Kentucky**, checking out the soggy horse farms as we made our way in and out of town, and a pit stop at a McDonald's in the vicinity of **Santa Claus, Indiana** (yes, Virginia, there is a Santa Claus in Indiana). We couldn't even tell you what the topography was like; all we saw was water. I nearly contracted vicarious tendonitis watching my wiper blades work overtime.

We stopped for the night in **Mt. Vernon, Illinois**, a town I'd never heard of which just happened to be in the right place at the right time. There have to be 5,000 hotel rooms in this town of only 15,000 residents. According to my iPhone, there are 31 chain restaurants within 0.83 miles of our boring five-floor Holiday Inn Express hotel. Never imagined so many people would come to spend so much time in so small a place with so little to do. But then again, here *we* are.

For those few of you who are Yankee fans (you know who you are), you will probably be buoyed (an appropriate word for the day) by the fact that I got to watch the second inning of the Yankees-Red Sox baseball game during our dinner break at a (chain) restaurant down the street (just past another six or so hotels). Emboldened by the fact that my Red Sox team is playing a lineup in which seven of nine players spent considerable time in Triple-A this season, you probably enjoyed watching us surrender three home runs in the second inning alone. It then got worse and we left the restaurant with burgeoning indigestion.

Here in Mt. Vernon we're now only about an hour and a half from St. Louis where we plan to spend the day (and night) tomorrow---unless it rains again and we float on by... And yes, there is a museum in tomorrow's plans: an encore visit to the venerable **Saint Louis Art Museum**. A full report in a day or two.

A Butt of a Different Color

Day 5 (Tuesday, October 2, 2012): Mt. Vernon, IL to St. Louis, MO (73 miles)

We escaped our second consecutive night in a Holiday Inn Express none the worse for wear and prepared for the short 73-mile trek to **St. Louis**. Speaking of wear: a strange vision as we gassed up before hitting the interstate: a big, fat guy dressed like a total slob wearing a dirty gray pullover with a big "Ralph Lauren" logo on the sleeve. Great advertisement for a fashion house. Ralph probably would have flipped over in his grave had he witnessed this extreme fashion faux pas. [Note: I'm informed by a source deemed reliable that Ralph Lauren is still alive. In that case, witnessing what we saw would have killed him.]

The ride to St. Louis was almost precipitation free, a big improvement over yesterday. Upon our arrival in the city, we headed directly for the **Saint Louis Art Museum**. This is a top-notch collection (free admission, free parking and a clearly-posted weapons-free policy) in a beautiful setting within a large urban park. Among the treasures of American art are a series of three mid-nineteenth century oils by Missouri artist **George Caleb Bingham**. The series' theme is the great American election process. As we anticipate the first presidential debates, it is curious to consider the artist's own description in 1854 of one of these paintings (and how well it would seem to apply to the upcoming debate):

In my orator I have endeavored to personify a wiry politician, grown gray in the pursuit of office and the service of party (Obama?). *His influence upon the crowd is quite manifest, but I have placed behind him a shrewd clear-headed opponent* (Romney, I presume, if you deem him clear-headed), *who is busy taking notes, and who will, when his turn comes, make sophisms fly like cobwebs before the housekeeper's broom.*

Then there was a 1991 "painting" by **Gerhard Richter** consisting of four sheets of glass, each quite large, each painted in an identical solid gray enamel. "In this work," bullshits the museum's curator on the wall label, "Richter upholds the possibilities of reflective illusions by denying personal artistic expression and the traditional materiality of painting." Sorry, but it is four identically painted sheets of glass playing a trick on pretentious museum curators.

Later in the afternoon we stopped at the nearby **Missouri History Museum**. Although they didn't have a plaque to celebrate the historic stupidity of Missouri's Republican senatorial candidate Todd Akin ("legitimate rape"), they did display various curious snippets from the past, some of which presaged the America of today. A mid-nineteenth century Missouri newspaper advertisement from a gun dealer, for example, proclaimed "Fire-arms--Fire-arms-- The country is safe so long as the majority of the western hunters, trappers and sporting patriots buy my Guns, Rifles, Pistols and Ammunitions: this question is settled."

The Gateway Arch reveals itself as we approach St. Louis

Museumed-out, we hopped into the car to check into our bed-and-breakfast for the night. We weren't more than a couple blocks beyond the museum, on a quiet road along the perimeter of St. Louis' genteel Forest Park, when something nasty caught our eye.

It was at least a three-quarter moon, if not a virtual full. There in the parking lane was a rather corpulent gent, seemingly middle-aged (though it wasn't his face I saw) hunched over the trunk of his car, displaying two enormous cheeks exposed to the heavens and earth. His pants (no Ralph Lauren logos were observed) were apparently no longer fully functional. My only regret is that I didn't have the gumption to pull over behind (no pun intended) him and snap (again no pun intended) a picture. For those of you who have been slogging through our blogs in prior years, you might recall that we had a similar experience at a gas station several trips ago. And no, this was not the same guy (today's was, to be blunt, a butt of a different color). Not sure how we manage to repel trousers, but we do seem to have that effect. It was definitely a sketchy sight.

From the ridiculous to the sublime: our B&B, **The Fleur-de-Lys Mansion**, is superb. Beautifully appointed, the restored Victorian mansion offers every conceivable amenity, from ubiquitous chocolates, chocolate-chip cookies, unlimited coffee, sodas and liqueurs to a high-definition television in our room which even includes the MLB channel (Major League Baseball for the uninitiated). The down side is that I've had to watch the Red Sox continue to embarrass themselves on national TV against the Yankees.

Finally, at the suggestion of one of our readers, we went to **The Hill**, the Italian section of St. Louis where baseball icons **Yogi Berra** and his childhood buddy and later longtime baseball broadcaster **Joe Garagiola** grew up, for dinner at **Charlie Gitto's**. This was a true old-line European-style restaurant with formal waiters and classic Italian dishes. The clientele was largely business groups, almost exclusively male, with only a few exceptions. The heavily-accented, much older (and homely) man in the booth behind us was dining with a much younger blonde whom, judging from a few snippets of overheard conversation, was not well-known to him. His long-lost niece? Ya think? Anyway, our meal was good, albeit expensive, and the service was fine if rather humorless. By the time we finished, it was again raining on the Hittners as we made our way back to the B&B for the evening.

Tomorrow, after what promises to be a full and delicious breakfast, we have a fairly long ride to Eureka Springs, Arkansas. Bet ya can't wait for our next report...

(Washing) Hands Across America (or Why Did the Cubans Steal My Sink?)

Day 6 (Wednesday, October 3, 2012): St. Louis, MO to Eureka Springs, AR (305 miles)

Following an indulgent breakfast of bananas royale french toast (burp!), we left our St. Louis B&B and headed southwest across Missouri and into northwestern Arkansas, with a brief stop in Cuba. **Cuba, Missouri**, that is, where we experienced a major advance in American restroom ingenuity (actually, British loo technology, as it turns out) during a bio-break at McDonald's. As each of us (in our respective restrooms, of course) prepared to wash up, we were initially flummoxed by the apparent absence of sinks. That's because they had been replaced with sanitation stations rem-

iniscent of something out of the Jetsons (for those of you for whom that reference is meaningful). To utilize these stations (which are cleverly embedded into the walls), you simply insert your hands. All of a sudden you receive a spritzing of soap followed by a sprinkling of water (during which period, according to the instructions, you are to embark upon the familiar hand-washing operation). The water then promptly stops and hot air cleverly blows down on your (hopefully rinsed) hands for several seconds. If all has gone as planned, you are able to remove your hands and marvel at their miraculously hygienic status. Of course if you're stunned by the whole experience, as we were, you are equally likely to remove half-soaked mitts with partially baked-on soap. Either way, as a McDonald's experience it is way better than the food (we only buy the dollar iced teas as I've indicated *ad nauseum*). One is tempted to predict that the ladies room in Cuba, Missouri will soon become a mecca for female rednecks who come to McDonald's to stick their heads into the wall for a quick and economical wash and blow dry.

Our objective for the day was the town of **Eureka Springs, Arkansas**. The first four hours of our drive was boringly uneventful. During the final hour, however, we negotiated our way through the **Ozarks** on winding, heavily rural, two-lane roads. The occasional vistas were verdant and beautiful. The road was mostly uninhabited except for a proliferation of churches of every imaginable denomination. The paucity of side roads made one wonder at the source of all these putative congregations. This, of course, was also redneck country, so every now and then one could see a nonsensical anti-Obama slogan plastered primitively

A view of downtown Eureka Springs

Old signage graces several old brick buildings in Eureka Springs

across a homemade sign or old auto carcass.

After checking in to one of the ubiquitous bed-and-breakfasts which dominate Eureka Springs, we toured the largely Victorian community, a one-time spa resort which now attracts tourists and retirees alike. The narrow local streets are filled with souvenir, clothes and craft shops which inhabit charming (and often kitschy) old stone, brick or wooden buildings from the late nineteenth and early twentieth centuries. For our Arizona readers, the look and feel is very much like the old mining town of **Bisbee, Arizona**. We were at a loss, however, to explain the proliferation of Corvettes making their way up and down the roadways. Later, our dinner waitress kindly explained that the upcoming weekend was the 22nd annual **Eureka Springs Corvette Weekend** during which hundreds of Corvette owners descend upon the community and drive aimlessly back and forth along the local streets. As best we could tell, a significant number of Corvette owners were already in town, presumably familiarizing themselves with the none-too-challenging two- or three-block downtown area so they wouldn't be overmatched when the brighter Corvette owners arrived later in the week.

If we survive tomorrow's abundant breakfast, we will head to **Bentonville, Arkansas** (about an hour's drive) to visit the **Crystal Bridges Museum of Art**, the brainchild of Walmart heir **Alice Walton** and undoubtedly the most important major museum to open in this country during the last several years.

*Peggy admires a vintage Corvette in town for
the annual Eureka Springs Corvette weekend*

Tales from Bentonville (or How I Was Outbid by a Walmart Heiress)

Day 7 (Thursday, October 4, 2012): Eureka Springs, AR to Tulsa, OK (163 miles)

Again, exhaustion has set in as we collapse on the bed in The Moroccan Room of our **Tulsa, Oklahoma** bed-and-breakfast. The connection between Tulsa and Morocco escapes me but the room seems comfortable enough.

The day began with another excessive breakfast, this time at our Eureka Springs B&B. We dined with an older retired couple, guests from Fayetteville, Arkansas. After the usual preliminaries, the wife asked me what I did prior to retirement. I gave a very brief (about four sentence) description of my life as an attorney to which she retorted: "That sounds boring." While I don't deny that, the rest of the discussion (with our host and hostess participating) was about how to control the deer population of Eureka Springs (prompted by the presence of four deer just outside the kitchen window). Now *that* was boring.

We headed out of town along a mountain road peppered with hairpin turns, stopping at **Inspiration Point**, a site about eight miles southwest of Eureka Springs with a breathtaking view of the **Ozarks**. What drew me to the roadside stop, however, was the absolutely stunning red 1955 Chevy Corvette parked at the Point (photo on preceding page). Not sure which sight I enjoyed the most. I recalled this vehicle as the most impressive car aimlessly parading through the streets of Eureka Springs the night before.

About an hour later we reached **Bentonville, Arkansas**, celebrated home of **Walmart**. I feared we'd encounter an army of Walmart greeters as we entered town but that was not the case. We were there to visit the **Crystal Bridges Museum of American Art**, a spectacular new museum (open less than a year) designed by the well-known Israeli architect **Moshe Safdie**. We've been looking forward to this, and planned our trip specifically to include this stop. The museum showcases a nearly encyclopedic American art collection assembled (largely in recent years) by Walmart heiress **Alice Walton**. While I had been aware of some of her acquisitions from the art trade press, Peggy and I were both blown away by the overall quality of the collection. It is hard to amass a great collection at this late date, even with unlimited funds, but Walton has made a terrific start. There are great examples from virtually every period: Copleys, Stuarts and Wests from the Colonial era; Coles, Bierstadts, Morans, Homers and Heades from the 19th century; Eakins, Chase, Sargent, Cassatt, Whistler, Remington and Bellows from the early 20th century; Hartley, O'Keeffe, Marin and Dove among the modernists and a handful of the usual suspects from the Abstract Expressionist and later

View, from outside of one of the galleries, of a portion of the new Crystal Bridges Museum in Bentonville, Arkansas

contemporary movements. And then there are some true gems by lesser known masters which were delightful (and unknown) surprises (e.g., a terrific Boston School portrait by the short-lived Boston artist **Dennis Miller Bunker**). There are wonderful Wyeths, a few Thomas Hart Bentons and an utterly spectacular Norman Rockwell depiction of *Rosie The Riveter* painted to celebrate the contributions of women on the home front during World War II. If there is any weakness, it is the relative paucity of western art (nothing at all was on view from the Taos School artists, for example). This is a well-designed, beautifully implemented museum, from the friendly staff (adapting the Walmart greeter philosophy to the art museum) to the inviting cafe (good food at reasonable prices, another apparent Walmart precept) and lovely grounds (which we, unfortunately, didn't have the time to enjoy). And to top it all, the museum is free (compliments, naturally, of Walmart). Except for the Walmart-phobic, this is a place well worth visiting, even if it is in Bentonville.

One curious coincidence: one of the artworks included in the museum's collection of representational art from the period between the two world wars was a small painting which Alice Walton apparently acquired at a Sotheby's auction in New York City two or three years ago. We had actually previewed that auction, made an appointment to view that and a couple of other paintings by the same artist and left bids on several of the works. I recall being stunned by the price eventually realized by the paintings at auction. So I guess we can say we underbid Alice Walton (though we weren't remotely close).

We wound up our visit to Crystal Bridges in the mid-afternoon and headed west to **Tulsa**, about two hours away. After checking into our B&B, we hightailed it to the nearest art museum, in this case the **Philbrook Museum** about a half-mile away. The museum, originally built as a residence in the 1920s by Tulsa oil baron **Waite Phillips**, replicates a Renaissance Italian villa and includes 23 acres of breathtaking gardens. The collection, seeded by Phillips' own collection and supplemented generously by other patrons since, contains some outstanding American and European works together with an eclectic mix of works from other cultures and many eras. Particularly significant is its collection of art of the American West and Native American art and crafts. The setting is lavish, both inside and outside, and we very much enjoyed the visit.

Rear view of the Philbrook Museum in Tulsa

For those of you who don't care about art, the foregoing reports were likely as boring as my career. I trust the rest of you may be motivated to visit one or both of these gems next time you happen to be, however inexplicably, in or near Bentonville or Tulsa.

Tomorrow we drop down to **Oklahoma City** and nearby **Norman, Oklahoma** where (guess what?!) we'll visit two more museums. This will bring our museum visits to seven for the trip, a new record for a Hittner cross-country jaunt. After that, we endure the intellectual equivalent of Walmart for three days as our route winds through Texas and New Mexico before we alight in Tucson (hopefully) by Monday night.

Copulating Cabs

Days 8 & 9 (Friday/Saturday, October 5-6, 2012): Tulsa, OK to Norman, OK (128 miles) and Norman, OK to Clovis, NM (388 miles)

For those of you who had feared (or perhaps hoped?) that we had fallen off the face of the earth, your prayers have been answered (for better or worse). Though as we sit here tonight in our **Clovis, New Mexico** hotel room, we are, at the very least, well off the beaten track. Here follows the skinny on our latest adventures:

Friday, October 5th: Tulsa, OK to Norman, OK (via Oklahoma City):

Who would have thought that you could see three outstanding art museums in two days in Oklahoma? Rhetorical question. But we did finish the art museum trifecta today with visits to the **National Cowboy & Western Heritage Museum** in **Oklahoma City** and the **Fred Jones Jr. Museum of Art** at the **University of Oklahoma** in **Norman, Oklahoma**. Both have outstanding collections if you are into western art. I'll keep it short, but for the particular benefit of our Southwestern readers who haven't been there yet, both museums get PAABAAMs! (i.e., Peggy And Art Best American Art Museum designations). In addition to a top-notch collection of historic western paintings, the NC&WHM has a large selection of outstanding works by the leading contemporary western artists comprised of the winning entries in the museum's prestigious annual **Prix de West** competitions. There are also displays of western artifacts, western movie memorabilia (from **Roy Rogers** to **John Wayne**), Native American cultural materials and a passable re-creation of a frontier town. The "Fred" was a decent if unspectacular college art museum when we last visited it two years ago but has now been dramatically transformed by its acquisition (jointly with the **Philbrook Museum** we visited in Tulsa last night) of the outstanding collection of (Dartmouth grad) **Eugene B. Adkins** consisting of western and Native American art, pottery and jewelry displayed in an entirely new wing built to accommodate it.

I'm tired from watching the Wild Card baseball playoffs so this is all you get for tonight. I'm signing off from the Legends Room in the **Montford Inn**, our Norman, Oklahoma bed-and-breakfast where the "attendant" (that's the best term I can use to describe her) responded to my inquiries about local restaurants with something like: "I have no idea; I'm new to this area. Just drive down the street and you'll see a bunch of them." Thanks. For you Yankee fans (as you contemplate the onslaught of the Orioles), you will appreciate that the Legends Room which we occupy is so named because it sports (pun intended this time) photos of famous (or infamous) Oklahoma athletes including Yankee stalwarts **Mickey Mantle, Ralph Terry** and **Allie Reynolds**.

Saturday, October 6th: Norman, OK to Clovis, NM:

After a breakfast nearly identical to the last two B&B breakfasts (square of some kind of egg thing, bowl of fruit, juice and tea or coffee), we began the long 380-mile trek across Oklahoma, through the Texas Panhandle and into the eastern end of central New Mexico. We were less than enthusiastic about the ensuing four-hour ride to Amarillo: we've endured this before and it has nothing to recommend it. But we elected to keep an open mind and go with the flow. As I-40 parallels much of old Route 66, we were drawn by a billboard advertising the **Route 66 Museum** in **Clinton, Oklahoma**. It was easy on/easy off, so we dropped in and spent about thirty minutes (and $8) plowing through middling displays and old photos relating, at least tangentially, to Route 66. There was a mock diner interior, three (and a half) classic cars and a hokey gift shop. Didn't seem significant enough to commemorate the old byway. No PAABAM for this museum. Of course when we returned to the interstate, we passed at least three more billboards luring equally unsuspecting motorists to makeshift Route 66 museums in at least three even more podunk Oklahoma towns further down the road.

A view of an exhibit at the Route 66 Museum in Clinton, Oklahoma

Peggy reminisces in front of another of the museum's exhibits

The ride through the **Texas Panhandle** manifests its own peculiarities. In **Groom, Texas**, alone, there is an elephantine Christian cross rising nineteen stories into the Texas skyline and an absurdly listing water tower (presumably known as the Leaning Tower of Groom) which is really just a contrivance intended to draw tourists to the tiny town of about 500 (it is even surmounted by a star which is lit up at Christmas time). There are billboards advertising Christian-themed attractions including the **Jesus is Our Lord Travel Center** and the **Top of Texas Catholic Superstore**. Then there was the ad on the local radio station touting the **Stuff-It Taxidermy Shop** where you supply the carcass and they return you the meat and the finished product, expertly stuffed. I kid you not.

Struggling to find a town large enough to furnish lunch (I guess we could have gone to the Stuff-It Taxidermy shop if all else failed), we made a brief stop in **Shamrock, Texas**, a rapidly declining burg along old Route 66. In addition to a couple of unappetizing fast-food joints, we passed several defunct restaurants before venturing into a rather sketchy wood-frame restaurant with a badly hand-painted "Texas BBQ" sign outside. There were only a couple of (equally sketchy) patrons loitering inside. Since I don't eat red meat, I stupidly asked an unshaven, somewhat dissipated-looking redneck whom I took to be the proprietor whether they had any chicken barbeque. His answer, a total *non sequitur*, was something like "we only make sandwiches on Saturday." That was enough for me and we left, deciding to persevere another hour and have a late lunch in **Amarillo**.

Continuing our search for new adventures, we departed Amarillo and headed southwest along a series of two- and four-lane rural highways which would take us through the last hundred miles of **Texas** and into **New Mexico**. This was a trip in every sense of the word. Our path took us along an intensely active railroad line (we passed at least a dozen and a half nearly interminable freight trains over the two-hour journey) which passed by an endless procession of humongous grain elevators (probably one every couple of miles), the skyscrapers of the Panhandle. At somewhat greater intervals were slaughter yards and meat-packing plants, each emanating a putrid and persistent stench. The town names (e.g., **Hereford, Bovina**) left little doubt as to their principal activities. We strayed off the road in one of the towns onto its main street. At 3 PM on a Saturday afternoon the few storefronts that weren't boarded up were already closed for the

The infamous "Copulating Cabs"

day. Perhaps the most unusual sight of the day was a white Mack truck cab hauling three identical cabs behind it, each propped behind the one ahead of it at a 45-degree angle. It looked for all of the world like copulating cabs (F---ing Trucking?). I always wondered where trucks came from and now I know.

We finally found our way to a seemingly normal Holiday Inn Express in one of the larger communities in the area, **Clovis, New Mexico**. A predominantly agricultural town, Clovis was the home of the **Norman Petty Recording Studio**, where **Buddy Holly** and **The Crickets** recorded some of their earliest hits (e.g., The Crickets' "That'll be the Day"). Just when we thought our adventures for the day had come to a calming conclusion, we went out to dinner at a nearby **Dakota's Steakhouse**. You might ask why a non-red-meater would go to a steakhouse after enduring the stench of slaughter houses all afternoon. Probably because it had chicken and fish on the menu and there was no place else to go. In addition to a disappointing dinner, we had a front-row seat to a veritable cultural smorgasbord. We were seated at the last open table, right beside a room divider behind which a group of about 25 were conducting a highly animated Baptist prayer meeting. This was an all-black, mostly female gathering punctuated by gospel solos and individual testaments of faith. On our side of the divider sat their cultural antitheses: toothpick-crunching white folks with boots and cowboy hats. While fried catfish was the dominant choice behind the divider, the redneck selection tended toward chicken-fried steak with mounds of heavily-buttered mashed potatoes. The guy next to us finished off his meal with a mouthful of smokeless tobacco *followed* by a swig of iced tea. Amidst this cultural incongruity sat Peggy and Art, liberals from the northeast, as divergent culturally as either of the groups adjoining us. The chance juxtaposition of all three of these cultural types was indeed a poignant reminder of this nation's enormous diversity.

Tomorrow we continue our descent into the heart of southeastern New Mexico toward the town of **Las Cruces**, probably our last night's stop before Tucson. Wish us luck!

No, this is not Noah's Ark. It is, instead, the place that cows go to stink and die. This was one of many such sights along the two-lane highways of rural New Mexico.

Little Green Men and Useless Las Cruces

Day 10 (Sunday, October 7, 2012): Clovis, NM to Deming, NM (362 miles, including Las Cruces detour)

Sunday, October 7th: Clovis, NM to Deming, NM (with a stop in a distant galaxy):

It seemed like a normal morning. We left our hotel in **Clovis, NM** and headed southwest, intending to finish the day in **Las Cruces**, at the southern edge of New Mexico. But to get there we had to go through **Roswell**, the (para)normal capital of the world. Aside from the little green men, it seemed like any other town. I can't remember much after that, except that we were transported in a silver, four-wheeled vehicle, a (Ga)Lexus, I believe, through a mountainous high desert moonscape, through unknown galaxies with strange names like **Ruidoso** and **Alamogordo**. And then, just as suddenly, we were beamed into a world of ubiquitous white sands piled high into endless dunes stretching out in every direction. We floated along a road carved out of the encroaching sands. It was an extraterrestrial wonderland! And as quickly as we arrived, it was over. We found ourselves mysteriously back in our own vehicle beside a sign announcing, in what seemed a remarkable coincidence, something called the **"White Sands National Monument"** somewhere on New Mexico Route 70.

Still stupefied, we continued our journey without additional extraterrestrial interference. And that's when things turned ugly. As we neared **Las Cruces**, we became hopelessly entangled in construction detours. We were directed to an exit for Las Cruces but it never materialized (or if it did, it was without benefit of signage). We found ourselves going east toward El Paso, Texas when we desired to go west to Las Cruces. After a ten- to twelve-mile detour, we extricated ourselves from the interstate and headed for an Italian restaurant which we had discovered on a prior trip through Las Cruces. We found the building but (surprise!) the restaurant was long gone. Consulting the iPhone, we located another branch of the eatery in another part of town. Naturally, dinner was less satisfying than anticipated. Afterward, we sought out a Hampton Inn listed in our

In White Sands National Monument, Alamogordo, New Mexico

purportedly up-to-date AAA guidebook. After driving past the address several times (and nearly running a red light doing so), we reluctantly concluded that the inn, too, was no longer in service. In total exasperation (and I'll spare you details of the venomous conversation), we decided we'd drive a few blocks to the Marriott we'd noticed during our unsuccessful search for the Hampton. Though we got tantalizingly close to the Marriott--it was actually *visible*--we found it impossible, in the confusion of lights, signs and traffic, to locate the damn entrance. When we turned into what appeared to be the only logical access, it turned out instead to be the on-ramp back to the interstate! Once again, the conversation degenerated considerably as we hurtled onto the highway, again rife with construction detours. Suffice it to say that I refused to turn back and we proceeded along the interstate heading for **Deming, New Mexico**, an hour west. Of course we were stopped by the Border Patrol on the way (though waved on upon our word that we weren't illegal immigrants). Upon our arrival in Deming we easily found and checked into a somewhat retro but seemingly serviceable Holiday Inn. The silver lining? The Holiday Inn in Deming was about $50 cheaper than what we would have paid in Las Cruces (and an hour closer to Tucson, to boot)!

Obviously, we're ready to get home. Three hours of drive time tomorrow morning should do it. None too soon, but (tonight excepted) it's been a lot of fun.

We're Back in Tucson!

Day 11 (Monday, October 8, 2012): Deming, NM to Oro Valley, AZ (230 miles)

In case you had feared that we had in fact been abducted by aliens in Roswell, we wanted to assure you that we arrived safely home in Tucson (Oro Valley) yesterday. Despite our travails in Las Cruces on Sunday night, we had a very enjoyable trip. It is good, however, to be back in Arizona, where summer weather continues unabated (about 90 degrees each of the last two days, more than 50 degrees higher than the lows we experienced in Arkansas, Oklahoma and New Mexico). We arrived to a renovated kitchen (which took a good chunk of the summer to complete) and the unwelcome task of repopulating the new kitchen with everything which resided in the old. We're very happy with the result but still struggling to learn how to work the appliances. Best of all, the cable works so I can watch the baseball postseason to my heart's content.

We hope you enjoyed our dispatches from the road over the past couple of weeks. If we didn't hear from you during that period, please drop us an email to let us know if you'd like to remain on our growing distribution list for our next trip in the spring. And in any event, please keep in touch!

www.ingramcontent.com/pod-product-compliance
Lightning Source LLC
Chambersburg PA
CBHW042228010526
44113CB00045B/2852